WOODBRIDGE
to the
COAST

ROBERT SIMPER

WOODBRIDGE TO THE COAST
Robert Simper

Published by Creekside Publishing 2008
www.creeksidepublishing.co.uk

ISBN 978-0-9538506-9-3

Printed by Lavenham Press

Cover.   A beef sucker herd grazing on the Kingston Marshes
Cover Back.   A Suffolk lane in May

Books by the same author:-

EAST ANGLIAN BOOKS

Over Snape Bridge (1967)
Woodbridge & Beyond (1972)
Suffolk Show (1981)
East Anglian Coast & Waterways (1985)
Suffolk Sandlings (1986)
Woodbridge: A Pictorial History (1995)
Suffolk: A Fine Farming County (2007)

SAIL BOOKS

East Coast Sail (1972)
Scottish Sail (1974)
North East Sail (1975)
British Sail (1977)
Victorian & Edwardian Yachting from Old Photographs (1978)
Gaff Sail (1979)
Sail on the Orwell (1982)
Sail: The Surviving Tradition (1984)

BRITISH ISLES

Britain's Maritime Heritage (1982)
Beach Boats of Britain (1984)

ENGLISH ESTUARIES SERIES

The River Deben (1992)
The River Orwell and the River Stour (1993)
Rivers Alde, Ore and Blyth (1994)
Essex Rivers and Creeks (1995)
Norfolk Rivers and Harbours (1996)
Thames Tideway (1997)
River Medway and The Swale (1998)
Rivers to the Fens (2000)
Up the River Deben (2006)

AUTOBIOGRAPHICAL

In Search of Sail (1998)`
Family Fields (1999)
Voyage Around East Anglia (2001)
Creekside Tales (2004)

COAST IN THE PAST SERIES

Forgotten Coast (2002)   British Isles
Sunrise Coast (2002)   Suffolk & N.Essex
The Lugger Coast (2003)   Cornwall & Devon
The Barge Coast of Suffolk, Essex and Kent (2007)

Chapters

'Bell and Steelyard' at Woodbridge.

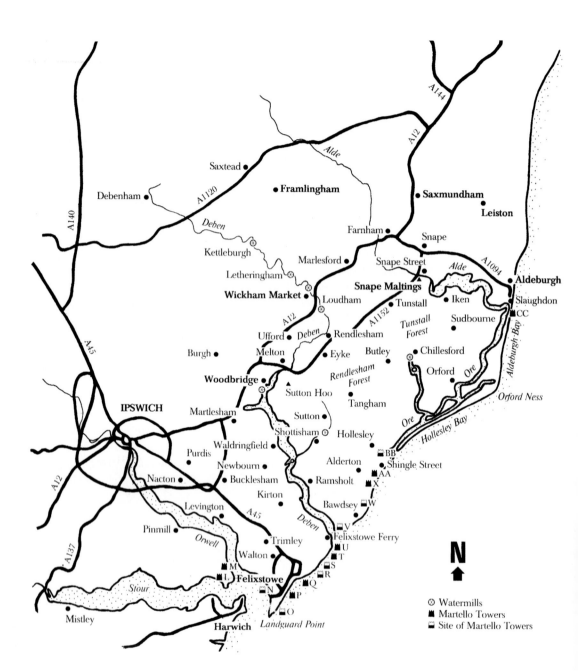

N

⊗ Watermills
⬛ Martello Towers
▭ Site of Martello Towers

Introduction

In 1968 when I started to research for *Woodbridge & Beyond*, which was in print for nearly forty years, I went to the Seckford Library on the Market Hill. The Library was quite small and the elderly librarian, Miss Redstone, was very keen to help with finding documents and then said 'one more question, do you have milk with your tea?' A few minutes later she appeared with cups of tea and cake for my wife and myself. This is the only time that this has happened to us in a library and it was a very pleasant act of kindness that seemed to typify Woodbridge as a friendly country town.

The Redstones, father Vincent and his daughters, were passionate about recording the past of Woodbridge. Vincent Redstone, a master at the Woodbridge School, started the Seckford Library in the 1930s in the former Seckford Free School, founded by Dorothy Seckford in 1666. All this is recorded in Carol & Michael Weaver's *The Seckford Foundation*. The Seckford Library closed in about 1972 and the material was moved down to the Suffolk County Council Library at the bottom of New Street.

I am grateful to Bob Merrick of the Woodbridge Museum, who has researched a great deal about the town, to Bill and Jane Kemball for letting me photograph Staverton Park and to Sam Newton for sharing his knowledge of the early history of the Sandlings. Angela Care Evans was responsible for the Sutton Hoo treasure while she was at the British Museum and took a leading part in two of the digs on the site and has covered the subject in *The Sutton Hoo Ship Burial*. To gain more insight into this fascinating subject there is Martin Carver's *Sutton Hoo: Burial Ground of Kings?* I drew on Carol Twinch's *The Little Book of Suffolk* for details of medieval saints.

On the Rivers Alde/Ore I have to thank Tim Miller and Christopher Parfitt. Robin Wright talked about Shingle Street and Stephen Worsley and Nick Rose about railways. John Kerr helped with the upper Deben and Margaret Booth-Smith went to a great deal of trouble to record details of the Deben Mill. Nicholas Longe assisted with Hasketon. In 1995 I wrote *Woodbridge: A Pictorial History* to cover the era of small businesses, with black and white photographs.

Every town and village on the Suffolk coast possesses its own strong identity. Orford still has a strong sense of being coastal Suffolk, although a great many new people have moved in. Aldeburgh is a place where the people who have moved in demand high standards, but are quite happy to pay for them. The great difference between 1968 and 2008 is that there are fewer folk to learn from who have been born and bred in the area. Fortunately I have recorded in my own notebooks many details of events which I would have forgotten over the years.

Although I continue to attempt to bring the atmosphere of a section of the East Coast alive, with words and photographs, my wife Pearl has been very much involved in shaping this book in every way. Diana McMillan, this time returning from sailing in Brazil, has skilfully undertaken the final edit.

RS
Ramsholt, 2008

Chapter One

Sutton Hoo
First Page of English History

An Anglo-Saxon battle being re-enacted at Sutton Hoo.

I first heard of Sutton Hoo as a schoolboy just after World War II, when my mother bought me a catalogue of the Sutton Hoo treasure from the British Museum. I found this very boring and could not understand the complex world of the Anglo-Saxons, but I was aware that something very important in early English history had happened very near to where I lived on the Suffolk Coast.

In 1939, on the edge of the Sutton Walks heath, just as the war clouds were blowing across the sea from Europe, a group of archaeologists unearthed a fabulous treasure that had been buried in a longship under a mound. This was one of a group of burial mounds on top of the hill overlooking the River Deben, across the valley from Woodbridge. It appears to have been common knowledge locally that there were ships buried under the mounds at Sutton Hoo, as treasure seekers had already raided the site. In 1911 a timber merchant built the great country house at Sutton Hoo and a small estate was formed in a corner of the vast area of heathland.

Colonel Frank Pretty and his wife Edith bought the Sutton Hoo Estate in 1926. Edith Pretty was known as the 'shipping heiress' while Colonel Pretty was a member of an Ipswich business family. Sadly, Frank Pretty died shortly after they moved there, but Edith continued living in the Sutton Hoo house and was a local magistrate. From the front room of her house Mrs Pretty could see the ancient burial mounds across a slight valley and she became very intrigued. Edith Pretty had visited the Valley of the Kings in Egypt and thought that there must surely be something of importance buried in the mounds. Once one of her friends, Doreen Cox, who was a houseguest, came down to breakfast and announced that she had a dream that a warrior was standing on top of the largest mound. Mrs Pretty took this very seriously because Doreen had 'second sight' and had predicted events in the past.

At the Woodbridge Flower Show in 1937 Edith Pretty asked the local historian Vincent B. Redgrave, who was a teacher at the Woodbridge School for 41 years, if he would dig into her mounds. Redgrave suggested that a dig at Sutton Hoo should be done correctly and recommended that Edith Pretty should contact Guy Maynard of Ipswich Museum. Although Maynard did not have the resources to mount an archaeological dig he presumed that anything of interest found there would go to Ipswich Museum. Maynard introduced Mrs Pretty to Basil Brown, a former land worker who had shown considerable talent in digging historical sites in Suffolk.

Mrs Pretty hired Basil Brown for the summer of 1938 and agreed that her gardener and gamekeeper could also help with the work of digging. Mrs Pretty wanted Basil Brown to dig the largest Mound One, but Brown wouldn't do this. He said he would start with the second largest, Mound Two, to learn how to handle the soil on the site.

In 1938 Brown's party discovered that Mound Two had been an Anglo-Saxon ship burial, but a robber's trench had destroyed most of the evidence. The few articles found were sent to Ipswich Museum and were later apparently lost. The following summer Mrs Pretty rehired Brown and he agreed to tackle Mound One. He started to dig a trench through the centre of the mound and almost at once found rivets that had been used to fasten the planks on a large clinker-built vessel. The acidic soil had completely destroyed the wood, but with great skill Brown retraced the shape of the longship in the soil. By mid-summer it was obvious that this ship burial was intact and the burial chamber in the centre of the vessel had not been robbed. For some reason – one of the greatest strokes of luck in English archaeological history – the western end of the mound had been moved or had eroded away. Perhaps the sand had simply been blown away in the prevailing south-westerly wind, with the result that when the robbers had sunk a hole in the centre they actually missed the burial chamber by a few feet.

Guy Maynard guessed that a major discovery was about to be made and started to ask around about

Mound Two at the Sutton Hoo burial ground originally had a great warrior buried in a chamber, with an up-turned longship above it. The mound was recreated to its original height in 1992 and it is being grazed by Norfolk long-horned sheep.

ship burials. He contacted a museum on the Isle of Man about a ship burial they had had there. In no time at all a buzz went around the archaeological world that something important was happening out on the heathland of East Suffolk. Charles Phillips of Selwyn College, Cambridge came over to have a look and was amazed at the sight of a huge longship being unearthed at Sutton Hoo. Phillips had the dig stopped by the Office of Works and quickly assembled a group of professional archaeologists to excavate the burial chamber in the centre of the longship. Poor Brown and his team were downgraded to barrowing soil away.

In the centre of the ship were the remains of a royal burial with all the items a great Anglo-Saxon leader would have needed in the afterworld. Fighting equipment, treasure to show his great status and everyday clothing. Edith Pretty phoned her dentist, Jack Rowbotham, and said 'you must come and see this!' He drove over at once and was absolutely amazed at the sight of golden buckle and plates being removed, and carefully recorded them as they appeared from the ground. Mrs Pretty and her friends sat on the side, in wicker chairs, watching the dig. Once, she had the dig delayed so that her friends who were attending a garden party could walk over and watch the progress.

Mrs Pretty's chauffeur, Lyons, had two nieces staying with him at Bromeswell and they also watched the treasure being unearthed. Elsie Lloyd recalled to Pauline Moore how they used to go up to Sutton Hoo every morning with their uncle, who had to wait to see whether the car would be needed that day. Basil Brown took a great liking to these two girls, as he didn't have any children, and invited them to go across to the site with him. The girls were there when the treasure was unearthed and they

J. H. Kemball & Son's Staverton Park is a very rare piece of ancient woodland and some of the oaks in the Deer Park are believed to be around nine hundred years old. After World War II, Government agencies tried to persuade Jack Kemball to clear the Park and farm it, but being such a unique place he decided to keep it.

handled the great bowls as they were passed around. The gold buckle sprang open when it came out of the ground. They also saw the place where the body had lain and noticed a thin layer of white power that just drifted away in the light wind. The body had been completely eaten away by the acidic soil. The girls were given a piece of cloth, but this quickly deteriorated.

The story of the Sutton Hoo discovery was kept from the public as long as possible, so that treasure hunters wouldn't raid the site. Mrs Pretty had an agreement with the *Woodbridge Reporter* that the news should not be made public, but Maynard leaked the story to the *East Anglian Daily Times* and then the London newspapers picked it up. The *Woodbridge Reporter* was a weekly paper and sadly its reward for keeping the secret was to be the last paper to report the major find at Sutton Hoo.

In August 1939, a coroner's court was held in the corrugated iron village hall at Sutton, to decide who could claim ownership of the treasure. A group of local worthies ruled that it belonged to Mrs Pretty and she promptly gave it to the nation. An extremely generous gesture, as this piece of early English history was priceless. The British Museum took charge of the Sutton Hoo treasure, much to the fury of Guy Maynard who had assumed it was going to the Ipswich Museum.

It is very likely that while the coroner's court was sitting there were other finds from Sutton Hoo sitting on mantelpieces in cottages in Sutton. Local people kept very quiet about the other finds. It would seem that two rabbit-catchers, Will Collins and his mate King, used to dig holes in the group of burial mounds on Sutton heath, if there was no one about, to find 'curiosities'. These were not sold, but kept as 'keepsakes' and seem to have been lost, or perhaps thrown away, over the years.

The Shepherd's Cottage in Staverton Park was probably built in about 1800 when sheep were still grazing the woodland.

What was the Sutton Hoo burial field about and who were the warriors buried here? Finds from the site were dated from around 625, which is approximately the same time as the death of Raedwald, the most important of the Anglo-Saxon kings of East Anglia. Raedwald was the most successful of the East Anglian kings of the Wuffings dynasty. As the Anglo-Saxons of the early settlement period didn't have a written language there is no definite proof that Mound One is the site of Raedwald's prestige burial, but evidence suggests that this was his final resting place.

It would appear that a group of Anglo-Saxon warriors under the Wuffings settled on the River Deben and, by the force of the sword, carved out the Kingdom of East Anglia which ran from the River Stour up to the edge of the Fens, roughly the same as the counties of Suffolk and Norfolk. The centre of the Wuffings early Kingdom, according to the Venerable Bede, was Rendlesham, a couple of miles up the Deben valley. The site has been field walked by John Newman and there seems to have been a very large Anglo-Saxon site covering about thirty acres. The Anglo-Saxons may have chosen this site, just inland, away from other raiding groups, because there had been a Roman farm here and a villa in neighbouring Campsea Ash. Each Anglo-Saxon king had a great hall, rather like a huge wooden thatched barn, and it is believed that Rendlesham Hall may be on the site of the Wuffings Hall.

Raedwald and his followers practised a pagan religion but they were in danger of being over-run by the powerful kingdom of Mercia that roughly covered the present day English Midlands. Raedwald needed friends and the King of Kent agreed to help him, if he converted to Christianity. Raedwald was baptised, but his wife and court would have nothing to do with the new religion from southern Europe and wanted to stay with the old gods from northern Europe. According to Bede, Raedwald solved the problem by having a Christian Church and a pagan temple beside it. Since the early English churches were sited on the old pagan places of worship there is speculation that Rendlesham Church could be on the site of the Wuffings temple.

There is no doubt that the present name of the river Deben comes from Debenham and does not go back much further than the eighteenth century. Tom Williamson believes the Wuffings took their name from the old Celtic word for the Deben meaning 'bending'. Certainly the fresh water river has more bends than other nearby rivers. The name lived on in Ufford, probably meaning the ford over the Wuff. The Kingdom of East Anglia may have started beside the Deben, but this was not a very central situation. The Deben valley didn't really lead anywhere and the centre of the kingdom probably switched to Ipswich, which had a valley leading up into central Suffolk. Later on Kings and then Earls of East Anglia were based in Norwich, by which time it had become a sub-kingdom of Mercia.

Sutton Hoo was forgotten and kept its secrets until the famous dig of 1939. Mrs Pretty, following her gift of the treasure to the nation, remained a respected member of the community. When I was young my family used to meet for lunch every Tuesday in Footman and Pretty's restaurant in Waterloo House, Ipswich. While we were quietly shown to our table there was always a tremendous fuss when Mrs Pretty arrived. The time of her arrival must have been known, as a senior member of staff used to show her to a special table next to the string quartet. I just remember Mrs Pretty as a rather gracious lady, usually dressed in a tweed suit, suitable for country wear.

Edith Pretty died in 1942 and the Sutton Hoo estate was sold to another, totally different, lady landowner. This was Mrs Martha Barton, whose great passion in life was showing British Friesian cattle, and she had no time for a 'lot of nonsense' about Anglo-Saxon kings being buried on her land. As the Sutton Hoo burial mounds were a Scheduled Monument she didn't touch them, but she showed her lack of interest by bulldozing out Hogg's earthworks, probably Iron Age, and had a silage pit dug as close to the monument as possible.

Because I was friendly with her son, John, I was invited to some of the parties at Sutton Hoo House. Martha Barton and her husband Jack, who had had a rather dashing career in the Royal Navy Little

Ships during World War II, were very welcoming, but I was aware of their lack of enthusiasm for local historical events.

When I heard that Rupert Bruce-Mitford was leading a British Museum dig on the Sutton Hoo Mound One in 1967, I decided that this was something to be seen. However neither the Bartons, nor the British Museum, were in the least keen for members of the public to visit the site.

Although I had lived in the area all my life I had no idea where the Sutton Hoo Mounds were. I picked a quiet time in the early evening and set off on the public footpath across the heath at Sutton Walks. To my delight I spotted the mounds, overgrown with bracken, and there in the centre of Mound One was the shape of the Sutton Hoo longship. I was deeply impressed by the size and shape of the ship. The original must have been a vessel of great beauty, but my thoughts were suddenly interrupted by the arrival of Ernie Collins, the Bartons' gamekeeper, with his shotgun resting on his bike's crossbar. He assumed, incorrectly, that I was a treasure hunter about to raid the site, so I left.

The sight of the Sutton Hoo ship's shape fired my imagination. In 1984, when I revisited the site with friends, I was a bit alarmed to see an authoritative figure moving hurriedly towards us. I expected to be swiftly removed from the area, but this turned out to be Martin Carver, who was about to lead a series of archaeological digs on the site. Far from sending us away, Martin invited me to join what became known as the Sutton Hoo Society, whose members are friends of the Sutton Hoo site. Martin told us his plan was to try and work out just what Sutton Hoo had been about, to 'unlock the mysteries of the past'. He also mentioned that part of the plan was to build a replica of the Sutton Hoo Ship and make a North Sea voyage. That was good enough for me. I was at the inaugural meeting of the Sutton Hoo Society at Seckford Hall.

Over the next seven summers Martin's team re-dug Mound Two, where they deduced that there had been a second ship burial, but in this case it had been upside-down on top of the burial chamber. Many of the other smaller mounds were also re-dug, only to discover robbers' trenches. In the last few days of the long series of digs they finally found a grave that had not been robbed.

Martin's version was that he hit a golf ball across the site and it bounced over a tiny bump. Could this be the remains of a small mound? The site had been swept by the wind for centuries and ploughed over on several occasions. The bump turned out to be what became known as the Prince's Grave. Here, a young warrior had been buried with all his fighting equipment, and a few feet away his horse was buried, about the size of a modern pony.

Over the decades attempts to start building a replica of the Sutton Hoo ship have been totally thwarted by academics disagreeing over just how it should be done. Tremendous academic discussions have gone into the possibility of building a replica longship, but nobody can agree. When I read that a replica of an Anglo-Saxon ship would be sailing in a traditional boat regatta at Henley-on-Thames I travelled up to see it.

This turned out to be the *Ottor*, a quarter-size replica of the Anglo-Saxon merchant ship found in a drainage ditch in Kent. It was being very capably sailed by Edwin and Joyce Gifford. With the Giffords I sailed quietly along the peaceful Thames in *Ottor*. They had thought of building a replica of the Sutton Hoo ship, but had heard of the academic opposition to the idea – even David Attenborough, representing the BBC, felt it was not necessary. Being chairman of the Sutton Hoo Society I suggested that a replica would be very welcome on the River Deben.

In 1994 the Giffords brought their *Ottor* to Suffolk and with Sam Newton, the charismatic academic who delights everyone by speaking Anglo-Saxon, we sailed up to Snape. The following year the Giffords returned with their new *Sae Wylfing*, a half-size replica of the Sutton Hoo longship, built by Geoff Bird, and given a name that Sam said meant 'Sea Wolf cub'.

In 1939 the lines had been taken off the shape in the mound of the Sutton Hoo ship, but these had been destroyed in the bombing during World War II. The lines were re-drawn by the British Museum from available information. It had always been believed that this was purely a rowing boat, but if this

Ramsholt Church stands in the centre of a mid-Saxon settlement and was probably originally in a woodland clearing. There are several churches in the Sandlings well away from settlements and the plague is usually the explanation for this. However, it is possible that the medieval landowners made clearances to make land available for sheep walks. Later on, more labourers were needed for arable farming and their cottages were scattered around the parishes.

ship had voyaged to northern Europe it surely would have had a sail for long voyages that could have lasted for weeks. Edwin devised a sail plan, based on Roman ships, and put a single square sail on *Sae Wylfing*.

In the Anglo-Saxon ship that was unearthed at Sutton Hoo in 1939 the burial chamber of the dead king was in the centre of the hull, exactly where the mast step could have been. No mast step was found, or indeed looked for, and it is assumed that the mast case was removed to construct the burial chamber. The other mystery was whether the ship had a side rudder. The only clue here was that the aft section of the ship had been strengthened, presumably to take the weight of a rudder.

The *Sae Wylfing*, on her frequent appearances on the Deben, proved to be very fast under sail when reaching, with the wind on her side. She will tack slowly against the wind in a moderate breeze, but it is easier to row her straight up into the wind. The Giffords and their loyal crew re-learned the art of handling a sail and oar longship. They also discovered that her long overhanging bow, which lifts the hull while sailing, was very useful for landing on a beach because it allowed the crew to jump out into shallow water or even on to dry land.

When the National Trust took over the Sutton Hoo Estate and work started on building the Interpretation Centre in the former kitchen garden, another Anglo-Saxon burial field was found. In 2000 the Suffolk Archaeology Unit excavated this site and found pagan graves of the period just before the famous royal burial field to the south.

In 2002 the National Trust opened their centre at Sutton Hoo and planned for 55,000 visitors in a year. In fact, during the first year there were 204,657 visitors, but this has levelled off to about 90,000 visitors annually.

The *Sae Wylfing* is a half size replica of the Anglo-Saxon longship found in Mound One at Sutton Hoo.

The clinker-built boats were introduced by the Anglo-Saxons and went on to be used in Suffolk for 1,400 years. In 1900 there were about three hundred clinker boats working off Suffolk beaches. The 15ft *Pet* IH45 was built by Bugg in a shed behind Sudbourne 'Chequers' in 1902. The 18ft *Three Sisters* IH81 was built in 1896 for Mr Ralph to fish off Thorpeness beach and Percy Westrup fished her here until about 1952. Both these rebuilt boats, the only two left sailing, were originally used for fishing off Thorpeness and Aldeburgh beaches.

The Suffolk beach boats *Three Sisters* **and** *Pet* **at Felixstowe Ferry.**

Chapter Two

A View of Woodbridge
Market Town and Port

The Woodbridge Shufflers 10k Run, passing the Shire Hall, Market Hill, 2008.

Michael and Carol Weaver at the Seckford Hall Hotel.

The Romans divided Britain up into provinces occupied by the Celtic tribes. The south side of Suffolk and Essex was the homeland of the Celtic tribe of Trinovantes and the local branch of this tribe probably had their 'capital' for south-east Suffolk at Wicklow Hill, Hacheston. The Trinovantes were mainly farmers while the Iceni to the north were mainly herdsmen.

During the Roman period Suffolk was developed as an agricultural area with a market economy. There was a large settlement, and possibly a fort, at Coddenham defending a crossing over the River Gipping and the road between Colchester and Norfolk. There was another large settlement at Hacheston on the road link to Coddenham and Knodishall. There appear to have been coastal forts at Dunwich and Aldeburgh and another, Walton Fort, at the mouth of the River Deben. The countryside was dotted with farms and small villas, particularly on the high ground along the Deben valley. It was an organized landscape that faded away once the Romans left in around 410.

The departure of the Romans and failure of the Romano-British to organize an effective army allowed the Anglo-Saxons, a mixed bunch of people from the tribes of northern Europe, to move in.

When the Anglo-Saxons settled on the Suffolk coast much of the land between the rivers was still ancient oak forest. The original settlers didn't like living in the silent and eerie forests, which they believed were the home of spirits, good and evil, and their first task was to begin clearing the trees. They either settled on land that the Romano-British had cleared or they exploited the woodland for building timber and for firewood. The forest re-growth could not keep up with demand, but someone with considerable authority stopped the villagers from clearing the 360 acre Staverton Park at Butley. The Kings of East Anglia at Rendlesham are the most likely candidates for this. Certainly the

The houses on Quay Side were built in the early 1500s, when Woodbridge was growing as a port. For about five hundred years Quay Side just led down to the quays and Tide Mill, but in 1976 the road was extended through to Lime Kiln Quay Road to relieve traffic congestion.

medieval forest became a hunting park for Butley Abbey and in 1528 Mary, Queen of the Scots, picnicked under the Staverton oaks while 'hunting of foxes'.

Later, Staverton Park and The Thicks became woodland pasture with animals grazing under the trees. Until the end of the nineteenth century sheep were grazed on the open 'sheep walks', the former forest, during the day and driven back to folds on the arable fields for the night. In this way the 'golden hoofed' sheep put nitrogen on the land and helped the grain crops. Once grazing stopped, in the nineteenth century, the 'bracks' (bracken) moved in.

It takes about twenty minutes, by car, to go from the silence of Staverton Park and The Thicks to the nearest Tesco superstore, but one has travelled forward in time about a thousand years.

Most of the village names in the Sandlings are of Anglo-Saxon origin. One such name is Kingston or Kyson, the headland between Martlesham Creek and the River Deben and this is believed to mean King's Town, so it is assumed that there was a possible connection with the kings buried at Sutton Hoo. No evidence has been found of any settlement here, but above Martlesham Creek, in the valley of the River Finn, there were many Anglo-Saxon settlements.

It is appropriate that Woodbridge Museum is on the Market Hill, because this is where the town of Woodbridge began. Possibly the settlement around the Market Hill started as a late Anglo-Saxon burgh. This was a feature of Suffolk and Norfolk – a very simple description would be a Lord of the Manor's compound. It would have had the Lord's Hall and his church and covered about 7 acres. Some burghs were larger and were fenced off with rather grand gateways. The fences would have kept out thieves, but not an attacking force. The villagers would have lived in huts scattered around the landscape, on land rented from the Lord.

A popular medieval female saint was St. Etheldreda. Etheldreda had been given the Isle of Ely by her father Anna, King of the East Angles, as a wedding dowry at her first marriage. According to Bede, she kept her virginity (and her dowry properties such as Ely) through two marriages. She led an austere life, eating one meal a day, praying and wearing woollen clothing instead of linen.

Before she died in 670, St. Etheldreda founded a monastery at Ely and this early association with the royal family of East Anglia resulted in Ely Abbey controlling a great deal of property in the Woodbridge area. In 970 King Edgar the Peaceable granted the manor of Kingston and the lands of Uderbryca (Woodbridge), Melton and Brightwell to Ely Abbey. This was part of the Liberty of St. Etheldreda (also known as the Wicklaw Liberty.) The Liberty was an area outside the jurisdiction of

The 'King's Head' on the Market Hill was built in about 1540. Percy Wix is standing in the door. He was born in the first house in Seckford Street in 1916.

a sheriff where dues or taxes were accrued by Ely Abbey.

In the medieval period many churches were dedicated to St. Etheldreda and her name was shortened to St. Audry. The old church at Melton, at the head of the tidal River Deben, was dedicated to SS Andrew and Etheldreda, but when the new church was built in about 1865 St. Audry was dropped because it was tainted by its association with the nearby St. Audry's mental hospital.

St. Etheldreda had suffered from a neck tumour, which she believed was a 'divine punishment' because as a child she had worn 'the needless burden of jewellery'. Necklaces and jewellery were sold at the medieval fair held on the Market Hill at Woodbridge on Audry's Day, October 23. This jewellery was rather tatty and gave rise to the word 'tawdry'. At the same Fair a Woodbridge baker sold gingerbread men for a farthing and eventually made a fortune. He went on to build Farthing Cake Hall just outside the town. This name was changed to Farlingay Hall and in the nineteenth century Edward Fitzgerald entertained Carlyle and Tennyson here.

In 970 King Edgar granted Woodbridge to Ely Abbey and this was the first mention of the name Woodbridge. It also appears as Oddebruge in 1050 and Wudebrig in 1205, which appears to mean a 'wooden bridge'. There was certainly not a 'wooden bridge' over the River Deben, but there may have been a wooden bridge over one of the small streams. This is not certain, but one candidate could have been a bridge at the bottom of Drybridge Hill over Steynings Brook. The main route into Woodbridge, until 1785, was along the high ground, down Drybridge Hill and into the Market Hill, past the 'King's Head'.

Ernaldus Rufus started an Augustinian Canon Priory at Woodbridge in 1193. In 1224 the Priory obtained the right to hold a market on the Market Hill to raise an income. The town, which hadn't become a port at this stage, grew up around this market. Most shipping had gone to Gosford, now King's Fleet, lower down the Deben, but as Gosford was a creek haven, not a town, shipping moved up to Woodbridge. The small Priory of the Black Augustinian Canons was never one of the rich and powerful monastic orders, and was among the first to be closed in the Reformation. In 1564 a private house, the Abbey, was built on the site of the Priory and this is now the Preparatory School for the Woodbridge School.

In the 1500s many of the timber-framed longhouses in Woodbridge went up and Leigh Alston believes that 1-5 Quayside, Woodbridge was originally an early 1500s warehouse, because this timber-framed building has stone walls. If Quayside was the area where ships discharged, the river

The Market Hill, Woodbridge, outside the 'Wild Strawberry' Cafe, 2008.

has been filled in to its present waterfront. The former 'Boat Inn', further along the street, was built in about 1530 and George Arnott believed it was always a public house connected with a ferry across to Sutton.

Over the centuries Woodbridge people have benefited from a charity, the Seckford Trust, which was started in the Elizabethan era. The Seckfords were a prominent Suffolk land-owning family based at Seckford Hall. Thomas Seckford was born in 1515 and became a successful lawyer in London. He was also Member of Parliament for Ipswich and held a position in the court of Queen Elizabeth I.

Elizabeth I hated the smell of new leather and once, when Sir Thomas Seckford attended her at court, she briskly remarked 'Fie, sloven; thy new boots stink'. Seckford used the remark to push home an outstanding point: 'Madam, it is not my new boots that stink, but it is the stale bills that I kept so long'.

Seckford owned a great deal of property, particularly in Clerkenwell in London and around Woodbridge. He was very much aware of the social problems of his day – poverty, old age and the lack of public education – so as he was childless he set up charities and used his wealth for the benefit of the people of Woodbridge.

Thomas Seckford, amongst his many legal public duties, was a Steward of the Liberty of St. Etheldreda and moved the Quarter Sessions from Melton to the Shire Hall, which he had built, on the Market Hill, in about 1575. The name Shire Hall was no doubt used because it was the justice centre for a 'county within a county'. The Shire Hall was the courtroom of the Liberty of St. Etheldreda. This was the centre of the Wicklaw, five and a half Anglo-Saxon Hundreds, which covered roughly the same area as the Sandlings branch of the Trinovantes tribe had occupied. The Wicklaw remained an administrative 'shire' until 1889, but some of the Liberty's officers were still in place at the beginning of World War I.

Originally the ground floor of the Shire Hall was opened for a corn market, but was closed when the building was rebuilt in 1864. In the 1930s my grandfather, Morris Turner, a farmer at Boyton, was asked to become a magistrate and he recalled feeling a bit awkward the first time he went because he was the only one on the bench without a title. In 1986 the Quarter Session was moved to Ipswich and ended the local expression 'going up the steps,' meaning that you had a summons to attend the court in the upper storey of the Shire Hall.

In the Elizabethan era Woodbridge took a great leap forward that began when the houses on the Thoroughfare grew up along the main road. Also, local men started building ships for London merchants. The important fact here was that there was a good supply of oak from the heavy land district around Framlingham. The town reached it height as a shipbuilding centre in the 1600s when it was supplying small ships for the Royal Navy. These were launched at Woodbridge, either at the Lime Kiln yard or into the Ferry Dock, and were towed to the Royal Dockyards at Deptford on the Thames to be fitted out.

The largest merchant ship launched at Woodbridge was the 700 ton *Goodman* in 1634, while the largest man-of-war was the 663 ton 4th rater *Kingfisher*, built by Edward Munday, on the site of the Riverside Theatre, in 1675. The final warships were the 5th raters *Hastings* and *Ludlow*, both of 381 tons and 32 guns, that appear to have been launched at the Lime Kiln yard. Although the Lime Kiln Yard was above the Common Quay (Ferry Dock) and the Tide Mill, it was on a bend in the river and had deep water where a ship could be launched easily. The Common Quay silted up and indeed is still silting up.

According to local legend, when ships were built at the Lime Kiln Yard their bowsprits went right over the 'Red Lion.' Maps show that the yard did go up to the Thoroughfare, but the top end was a timber store. The slipway from which these large vessels were launched would have run down into what is now known as Gladwell's Dock. The 1992 flood defences in this Dock have covered up the small Tudor bricks. Presumably this dock was constructed when the merchant ships were being built here in the Elizabethan era. Linked to the shipbuilding was the manufacture of sailcloth. This started in Woodbridge in about 1575 and there were around ten weavers working in the town until the end of the 1600s. The cloth was made from hemp grown on the lightland in the coastal villages. Both shipbuilding and sailcloth manufacture continued after this, but never on quite the same scale.

Other crafts that gave employment in the town were wool-combing for spinning and hat and rope-making. Woodbridge Salt was one of the town's main exports, made in saltpans near the Ferry Dock. The Woodbridge salt and Suffolk cheese were taken by coastal vessels to London. The cheese was mostly made in High Suffolk in the Dairy Lands and had a reputation for being very hard. Even the sailors in the Royal Navy refused, at times, to eat it. Daniel Defoe summed it up as 'Suffolk makes the best butter and the worst cheese'.

Woodbridge settled down as a market town and port and was only disturbed when troops were garrisoned here. Troops were first stationed in Woodbridge in 1750, and there were also camps on Bromeswell heath, above the 'Cherry Tree', of about a thousand men with 600 'camp followers', women and children, living in turf huts nearby. During the Napoleonic Wars, Ipswich and Woodbridge became garrison towns. The plan was that if the French invaded, the troops would be dispatched to fight them. The roads across many Suffolk heaths, then open sheep walks, were straightened so that they could march quickly to intercept an invading force. In 1805 a new road was also constructed making a straight route between Woodbridge and Melton.

In about 1805 troops were billeted in wooden barracks just to the north of the town near Drybridge Hill. There were about 700 cavalrymen and 4,000 infantrymen housed there. The brewer, Cordy,

Bernard Barton, the Woodbridge poet and clerk at Alexander's Bank, was buried here in 1849, in the Quaker's graveyard, in Turn Lane, Woodbridge.

delivered 635 gallons of beer to the barracks each day and there was a great deal of drinking and fighting in the town. The vicar became very busy with marriages and births.

The Cavalry officers used to go hunting and it is recorded that they killed a stag at Kesgrave. In the evenings Grand Balls were held in the 'Crown' Assembly Rooms, and the Fisher family, who operated a series of small theatres, had one built in Theatre Street. The western end of the Thoroughfare was renamed Cumberland Street after the Commanding Officer, the Duke of Cumberland. Speculators put up houses for officers to rent and many Elizabethan timber-framed houses were given more fashionable Georgian frontages. While enterprising tradespeople made money out of the troops, the Quakers and other chapel-goers found their drinking habits very hard to put up with. Celebrations were held at the end of the Napoleonic Wars for a victory over the French and the local people were also delighted that the troops were leaving. The barracks were pulled down in 1815 and the materials sold. The numerous pleasant houses in the town attracted 'gentlemen of means' to come and live in Woodbridge and this set the character of the town for the future.

The threat of invasion saw Martello Towers being built along the coast in about 1812. These were built with bricks, probably from Grays on the Thames, and delivered by sailing barges on to the open beaches during the summer. The troops manning the Martello Towers lived back from the sea and cottages were built for them in Bawdsey, Hollesley and Shottisham.

The high wheat prices at the beginning of the nineteenth century saw the port of Woodbridge and the villages in the Sandlings prosper. As the centre of a major grain-growing area it is not surprising that the majority of the important old buildings in Woodbridge were connected with the corn trade. The Shire Hall was a corn exchange, the 'Bell and Steelyard' was used for weighing wagons before and after going down to the quays and the Tide Mill was used for milling corn to be shipped away. The Steelyard was added to the 'Bell Inn' in about 1680 and was capable of weighing a loaded wagon of two and a half tons, and was in use until about 1885.

In the nineteenth century the port of Woodbridge was slowly robbed of its trade by Ipswich. The greatest problem was that the upper reaches of the river were silting up and there were also difficulties getting ships in over the shallow shingle bar at the entrance to the River Deben. However, there was trade and about thirty-six brigs and schooners were owned, and mostly built, in Woodbridge. The main imports were coal from the north of England and timber from Scandinavia. Ships couldn't

The 'Crown' and the 'Cross', Woodbridge, 2008. The 'Cross' has 'established 1653' on it while the 'Crown' may be older. In the eighteenth century the Prince Regent used to stay at the 'Crown' while on his way to shooting parties at Sudbourne Hall.

always get up to the Woodbridge quays so they lay at anchor in Kyson Pool, just down river from the town, and part of the cargo was brought up river in small barges. When the ship's draft had been reduced they then sailed around the corner, past the granary on stilts, in Granary Reach, and finished discharging at Woodbridge.

The best known of the Woodbridge tops'l schooners was the *Bernard Barton*, named after the town's famous poet and, when she sank in 1899, she was the last Woodbridge trader afloat. When the *Bernard Barton* was launched in 1840 she was one of twenty-three similar vessels from the Lime Kiln yard. The schooner *Ellen*, launched in 1853, was the last wooden trading vessel built at Woodbridge.

Woodbridge continued as a port with some 20,000 tons a year going over her quays. It was also the port of registration for the Rivers Deben, Ore and Alde and a total of some seventy vessels amounting to 5,000 tons were registered here. In 1882 Woodbridge ceased as a Custom's Port and the Woodbridge fishing boat registration letters WE were lost so the local fishing boats took on the Ipswich letters IH.

In 1794 one coach and a carrier wagon a week passed through Woodbridge and it took thirteen hours to reach London. By 1844 twelve coaches, omnibuses, carrier's wagons and carts were passing through the town daily on their way to London. There was also a steamship service, started in 1842, with the *Eclipse*, which ran from Kyson Quay to London.

In 1856 the railway line between Ipswich and Lowestoft reached Woodbridge and cut right through the quayside area. There were people in the town who tried to fight off the railway tooth and nail. Where the Riverside Theatre stands, Smith had been running a boatyard, no doubt the remains of the shipyard where the *Kingfisher* was built. This yard closed down as it became cut off from the river. The ancient saltpans, once one of the town's main industries, were also filled in. Some protesters just couldn't see the point of railways, but it must have made life a lot easier when it arrived.

The 5,000 population of Woodbridge had been falling but the arrival of the railway stabilized the situation. Some new light industries grew up, and the population stayed about the same. Many people believed the arrival of the railway would mean the end of the port of Woodbridge and the town's businessmen were very reluctant to invest capital in shipping or improving the quays, but the railway and barge traffic co-existed for another sixty years. Railways were very expensive to maintain and small sailing vessels were able to undercut them for bulk haulage of coal, grain and other basic commodities.

In 1883, 346 sailing ships and three steamers brought 22,968 tons to Woodbridge and the port was probably saved by the flat-bottomed sailing barges, which could get up the river more easily than deep draft schooners. As no barges were built in Woodbridge, shipbuilding died out completely, but several were owned here. Captain Read owned the round-sterned, tiller-steered *Deben* built in 1874 and this served the town as a 'hoy'. These craft ran a regular service to London with small consignments of freight.

Just getting barges up to Woodbridge was a major task. In 1879 there were seven pilots at Felixstowe

The 'Anchor' Pub at the bottom of Quay Street

The 'Woodbridge Mariner' on the end of one of the Ferry Dock warehouses.

Ferry and they brought in fifteen to twenty craft a month and went fishing in between jobs. The shortest time a barge stayed in the river was four days, but it often took two weeks before they left the river. One of the economic difficulties of the Deben was that there were very few freights out of the river once the Waldringfield cement factory closed.

The spritsail barges had little difficulty beating up the open river to Ramsholt, but the big boomies had trouble sailing even here. Arthur Hunt once told me how, as a boy in around 1900, he had seen the boomie *Susie* fail to come about just above Ramsholt Dock and she ploughed up on to the mud in front of the church. One of the mates on the boomies, 'Tricker' Finlay had such a difficult time getting a boomie up to Hart's Dock (now Gladwell's) that he swore 'may this dock fly afire before I ever come here again!' He was knocked overboard by the boom and drowned off Harwich on the next trip.

Having local knowledge of the river must have been a great help. Captain Douse traded here for years with the tiller-steered 85ft boomie *Empire of India* bringing coal from Seaham to the Tide Mill Quay at Woodbridge. The Woodbridge pilots were respected by bargemen because of their ability to get craft up safely. On small neap tides they took barges up to Melton Dock, built in 1793, and on high spring tides to Wilford Bridge Wharf, built in 1840. Melton Dock had barge traffic until about 1928, and barges took stone up to Wilford Bridge for road-making for a few more years.

There were about eight Woodbridge pilots and hufflers. The pilots, who were told by merchants when a vessel was coming, used to stand at a gate on the Warren Hill and look down river with a telescope. In fine weather they could see the barges' topsails as they came in over the Deben bar. This was before 1916 when Quilter had the trees planted on the Cliff in the Rocks Reach, to provide work for local fishermen.

The pilots judged when a barge would be at Bowships, below Waldringfield, and rowed or sailed down the river to meet it. If the wind was down the river and they had to tack, an extra 'tidesman' went as well and he stood on the bow with a 'setting boom' to push the bows off the mud when they were trying to turn. One of the pilots' skiffs has survived, the clinker 12ft *Teddy*, which was built in a shed at the bottom of Brook Street in 1877 for the pilot Sam Marsh. Building fast clinker rowing boats seems to have been a speciality for Woodbridge boat builders.

When the Kent barge *Youngarth* came up in 1920 with bricks, her skipper was very pleased that she came around each time and the two Woodbridge men didn't have to use poles. Deep draft vessels, such as the schooners that brought timber from Scandinavia, were charged more by the pilots. The worst place was Troublesome Reach where the wind blew straight down Martlesham Creek and there was a shallow patch in the middle. In 1879 Loder's Cut was dug here, for £250, to create a short cut to the Woodbridge quays. A Jetty was built in deep water outside the coal yard, near Everson's yard, on the site of the granary on stilts. This was used to save the time spent getting up to the Ferry Dock or round the bend to the wharves near the Lime Kiln yard. The barge owner Captain Robert Skinner was in partnership with the coal merchant, Cox. Skinner's boomie *Lord Alcester* used to bring 290 tons of coal to the Jetty, but his attempts to keep the barge trade going failed and his last trade was bringing shingle from the Deben bar, to build the new Woodbridge bypass, in his barges *Dover Castle* and *Tuesday*. Barge trade ended in 1935 when Skinner was found dead aboard the *Tuesday* off Green Point. However, in 1935 there was another venture to start a shipping company at Sun Wharf with small Dutch motor-sail coasters. Coasters used to bring dried peas and coal up to the Woodbridge Canning Co. warehouse at Sun Wharf until 1940. The last freight was held up by ice at Waldringfield.

Chapter Three

Gentle Market Town
Light Industry and the Café Society

Hamish Alexander and his father, John K. Alexander, outside Alexander's, in the Thoroughfare, 2008. The Alexander's shop opened as a Men's Outfitters at No. 51 The Thoroughfare in 1927 and moved to No. 10 in 1945. In 1977 they bought Dewhurst's butchers shop, next door.

Andy Seedhouse in his Boat Sale office. This was originally the Woodbridge office for Eastern Counties Farmers when they had warehousing on the Ferry Quay. Andy started Boat Sales here in 1977 and his son James joined him in 1990.

In the nineteenth and early twentieth centuries the shops in Woodbridge depended on people coming in from the surrounding villages. Those who did not have their own horses came on the weekly carrier's cart or walked. Some from the Sandlings took a short cut across Sutton Heath and came over Sutton Ferry, which ran every day of the year except Christmas Day. Woodbridge's Thursday Market on the Market Hill petered out in 1919, but the chicken sales went on a little longer.

If the housewives couldn't walk all the way into Woodbridge then shopkeepers sent their vans out to the villages. Tysons, grocers in the Thoroughfare, had a fleet of vans in the 1930s, and no cottage was too remote for them to visit. There were also tailors and other tradespeople who travelled out to the villages, selling goods and getting orders.

People going to Ipswich would walk to the ferry at Ramsholt. The Kirton farmer and baker, Fred Cordy, used to take the Ramsholt foot ferry across the Deben every week and deliver bread around the village. The Ramsholt ferry probably closed when Quilter opened a chain steam ferry at Bawdsey, which ran between 1897-1931. Local people then went shopping in Felixstowe. The Alderton butcher, Jack Garrard, also delivered his meat to the cottages. He had a paddock just up the Hollesley road from his shop on The Knoll and every week he drove two steers, two sheep and two pigs down to the slaughterhouse beside the shop and pole-axed them. Butchering, cutting up the animals, was very hard work and slaughtering ended here in 1946.

In World War I the Essex Royal Horse Artillery was again billeted in the Woodbridge School

The Excelsior Band playing at Woodbridge Regatta.

The Thursday Market at Woodbridge.

The attractive station at Woodbridge dates from the period at the end of the Victorian era when railway companies were seeking to standardize the railways.

The 'Waterfront Café' in the ground floor of the Granary on Tide Mill quay, Woodbridge, 2005.

grounds while training for trench warfare. The soldiers went to the 'King's Head Inn' on the Market Hill, where the main room became known as the 'slaughter house' because there were so many fights there, between the soldiers. One morning the landlord's son picked up seven teeth in the yard at the back!

In a small community like Woodbridge there were lots of rivalries and it was said that at any one time half the town was not talking to the other half. There was great rivalry between those who attended the Church of England and the others who went to the various chapels.

Some tradesmen had rowing boats and on Sundays, their only day off, they rowed their families up or down the river with the tide. Pleasure boating at Woodbridge had begun in the 1740s and in 1756 a 21ft 'pleasure boat' was auctioned at Orford Quay. The first report of racing on the Deben appeared in the 'Ipswich Journal' in 1783 when the *Templer* and *Flora* raced from Woodbridge to Bawdsey Ferry and back for a 'valuable silver cup'. However the reason it was reported was because some unsporting person stole the cup!

To celebrate the Coronation of Queen Victoria a Regatta was organized at Woodbridge in 1838. In the yacht race the *Elise* from Manningtree won, and Captain William Trott, a ship-owner living in Quay Lane, came second with the yacht *Pleasance*. The other races were held for four-oared and for two-oared boats, as rowing was an important local sport. But it was not until 1896 that the first Woodbridge Rowing Club was formed. The early regattas were tremendously popular and about 4,000 people, including passengers brought by steamers from Ipswich, came to watch the boats racing.

A Suffolk horse from the Hollesley Bay stud at the opening of the restored Tide Mill Quay, 2005. The Suffolk horses have powerful necks, and can pull twice their own weight.

The regatta led on to the formation of the Deben Yacht Club, the first Club on the river. The first yachts in the club were about 20-21ft long and were gaff cutters with loose-footed mains'ls. One of these, the *Helen*, achieved national recognition when she was sailed to Holland in 1851. It was about this time that another Woodbridge yacht owner, Edward Fitzgerald, started to receive national acclaim with his translation of the Persian love poem 'The Rubaiyat of Omar Khayyam'. Fitzgerald, an eccentric gentleman of means, had a 38ft schooner built in 1863. He named this yacht *Scandal*, which he claimed was the 'staple product of Woodbridge'.

The Woodbridge chemist, Gall, had the 30ft yacht *Syren*, built at Woodbridge in 1842, and she carried a small cannon, used to start the races. He also had a paid hand, a one-legged man called 'Peg' Grey. The yacht didn't have an engine so no doubt Grey sometimes had to row her home. The *Syren* was based at Woodbridge for seventy years and made one voyage to Holland. Once, Gall got into difficulties coming across the Deben Bar and after this he stayed in the river.

By the 1890s Ipswich had taken most of the Woodbridge port's trade and also the corn and cattle markets. The town's councillors, very much influenced by the yachting gentry, saw that the future of the Deben was for leisure. The railway had already sliced through the quayside area and the old salt

Re-launching the 12ft Woodbridge pilot's boat *Teddy* at the second Maritime Woodbridge, 2007. This boat was originally built for the pilot Sam Marsh in 1877. His grandson, John Marsh, is standing with his son and grandson Sam. The shipwright Lawrence Hebson, on the left, restored the boat,

warehouses had been pulled down. The warehouses on Jessup's Quay, on the downriver side of Ferry Dock, were very run down and these were demolished. A beach was created for the children to swim from and a wrought iron shelter was put up. This created the River Walk where the townspeople could promenade along to the bandstand, near the Jetty.

Woodbridge had some homegrown local light industries. A.V. Robertson came over from Ipswich to run the Lime Kiln yard when his father bought it in 1884. Plans of the big wooden sailing ships that had been built there in the past were stuffed in the loft above the office, but Robertson's concentrated on building yachts.

Robertson once complained bitterly to the owner of a yacht that he had just launched: 'I lost money on building this boat, in fact I have lost money on every yacht I have built'. 'Well Mr Robertson' replied the new owner 'you must have had a tidy pile of money when you started'.

Several of the shipwrights who had apprenticeships at Robertson's went on to start their own yards – Everson down near the Jetty, Claude Whisstock on some marshland between the Tide Mill Way and the Ferry Quay and, after World War II, Frank Knights had his yard on the Ferry Quay.

Woodbridge Canning Company put up a factory in the town, Girdlestone made pumps and there

'The Tea Hut' café on the River Walk, Woodbridge was reopened in 2007

Richard and Alison Youngman in the Grange Farm Shop, Hasketon. During World War II the Tile Bros. were running a vegetable washing plant in Station Road, Woodbridge. Fred Tile bought Grange Farm and planted apple trees. In the 1950s a new pack house was put up and from September to April their apples and Henry Foskett's potatoes were sold from here. This was one of the first farm shops in England and after Fred, died his wife Lillian and daughter Mary used to run it.

Nicholas Longe took over the apple sales in about 1973 and became a very large retailer, but foreign imports began to destroy the apple trade. In 1995 Richard and Alison Youngman, who already had an orchard farm, took over and greatly increased the range of goods in the shop. They have been able to do this because more and more small-scale specialist growers began producing vegetables and other products. Sadly, because of foreign imports, most of the local orchards have been 'grubbed' out.

Joyce Williams outside R.F. & J. Williams general stores, Grundisburgh, 2008. Ray and Joyce Williams started an electrical goods shop around the corner in 1954 and moved to the old Post Office on the Green in 1968. All four of the Williams daughters are involved with the shop. The eldest daughter Claire opens 'the shop that has everything' four days a week. Julie keeps free- range pigs and provides the meat and sausages to be sold in the shop. Rosie opens the shop on Saturdays and Diana makes the collectors' teddy bears.

Blacksmith Terry Pearce at Bredfield, 2008. Most country blacksmiths' shops depended on shoeing horses an making ironwork for farms, but when Terry's grandfather started at Bredfield in 1919 decorative wrought iro work was developed and this side of the business has continued.

was a brushworks in Church Street, while the Tile brothers had vegetable-cleaning sheds in Statio Road. There was a steam mill in Quayside and a maltings at Melton Hill. Potters garage was at th north end of the Thoroughfare and there was another garage in Cumberland Street.

All the road traffic from London to Great Yarmouth used to pass through Woodbridg Thoroughfare. This included the lorry that raced from Yarmouth to Billingsgate Market, at nigh with fresh fish. Once, going down the hill at Martlesham, just before Robert Finch's blacksmith shop the lorry failed to get round the corner and crashed into the hedge. This caused some concern an someone suggested that in order to make it easier to see the corner, a white line should be painte down the middle of the road. According to local tradition, this was the first time that a white line ha been painted on a road in Britain

The white line may have helped, but it did not solve the problem of increasing road traffic throug the narrow Thoroughfare. In the early 1930s a new by-pass road was built to the north west of th town and this was widened in the early 1960s.

During World War II most local men left to fight in the armed forces, but once the United States joine the allies in their fight against the Nazis in 1942, a quarter of a million US servicemen moved into Ea Anglia. There were about 108 airfields and it is said that you were never further than five miles awa from a US Air Force base. These airfields were built at great speed, carved out of fields and farms t machines that amazed the rural community. It opened their eyes to the future use of machinery.

The 820th Engineers, a black regiment, built Debach airfield in 1943-44 in record time. Two concrete roads were built at Shingle Street so that lorries could load up shingle off the beach. This was probably done too quickly and so much driftwood went into the Debach runways that they broke up. Away from the harsh business of the war the American servicemen, 'The Yanks', drank most of the beer in the pubs and according to local legend, were entertained by Glen Miller and his band in the 'Crown' Assembly Rooms.

The first USAF plane arrived at Bentwaters Air Base in 1943, on the runway built with shingle from Benacre, which was all brought over the humpback bridge at Snape. Most of the Suffolk USAF bases had Flying Fortress bombers, known as the Silver Fortresses. They were silver because they had not been painted, as it was believed that the war was not going to last long. The USAF daylight bombing, which gave them a one in three chance of returning, was calculated to make greater impact and shorten the war. One day in 1944, 1,400 bombers and 700 fighters took off for one raid on Germany.

The American servicemen left just after World War II, but when the Soviet Union showed signs of moving further across Europe they returned for the long, peaceful, Cold War and the last USAF aircraft took off to return home in 1996.

During the fifty years that the USAF was in East Suffolk many servicemen married local girls, so today many Suffolk families have relatives in the United States. In 1992 I met a World War II USAF serviceman in Lavenham who had married a girl from Southwold. As a young man he had ended up working on the USAF graves at Cambridge. He survived by simply blotting out the thought of all the young men he was burying. When he returned he realized how beautiful Suffolk was, particularly the churches. He had not noticed any of this before and also commented on how much the wealth and standard of living had risen in England.

In the 1950s Woodbridge was still a quiet country town with shops in the Thoroughfare and Market Hill owned by local people who had often been there for several generations. Although the Thoroughfare became one-way in the 1950s, it was still possible to drive along it and park beside the road. As the traffic up Church Street and down New Street increased, a new road was built at the bottom of Elmhurst Park in 1973, even though there had been a campaign to stop it because it was felt it would 'ruin' the park.

As new housing developments have been going up around Woodbridge all the time the number of people using the town centre has increased. In 1983 the Turban Centre and a car park were opened. The lower end of this was on the site of the former Woodbridge Canning Company, whose brand name had been Turban. Many of the old family-owned shops such as Hasnips, the electrical suppliers in the Thoroughfare, closed and in 1992 Rushbrooks, the china and household goods shop in Church Street, shut down. This was regarded by many, at the time, as being the end of the old-style shop era.

With car ownership becoming widespread, people travelled to work in Ipswich or Felixstowe or even London but enjoyed returning to their homes in Woodbridge. At the same time industry was moving out of the narrow streets to Melton, Martlesham Heath, Jolly's Sluice Farm beside Martlesham Creek and other workshops out in the villages.

In the 1950s places for eating out were very limited, mainly 'Seckford Hall', 'The Bull' and 'Crown' Hotels. There were also fish and chip shops at the bottom of New Street, Crown Point at Martlesham, the Horse & Groom corner in Melton and one in the centre of Wickham Market. By 2000 the café society had taken root in Woodbridge with over twenty-two widely different restaurants, cafes and fast food takeaways. Some eating-places even had chairs on the pavement, which would have been unthinkable forty years before.

The cinema was started in 1915 as the Woodbridge Electric Cinema, because there were so many troops in the town. It had been purpose built with 615 seats, on the site of store sheds. By the 1980s the cinema had become very run down and the screen had a patch in it that, according to local legend, was where 'the soldier threw his boot'. In 1985 Pat Betts bought the cinema to save it from closing.

The sailing barge *Victor* at Woodbridge Tide Mill Quay.

Shottisham Mill finished working in 1952 and was converted into a house in 1985.

It was refurbished with 264 seats, renamed The Riverside Theatre and opened with a new restaurant. Stuart Saunders, then just twenty, came to manage the new venture and has bought the whole business gradually over the years.

  Woodbridge stopped being a country market town in the 1960s and gradually moved on to become a residential centre and a town that people love to visit. Woodbridge is in the golden triangle of high employment with Felixstowe, the Port of Felixstowe and Ipswich. This has not escaped the notice of the outside world. Woolworths came to Woodbridge many decades ago, but it was not until 2007 that national chains began to move in. Costa Coffee were not sure whether Woodbridge was ready for the café society, but it worked well so they decided to look for a site in Aldeburgh. W.H. Smith & Son and Laura Ashley came to Woodbridge because it was a successful, lively community which is exactly what Thomas Seckford, who lived in a house off the Market Hill, plotted when he made it the capital of a special little shire.

Suffolk wagon and scythe. Farmers rarely throw away their old 'implements' so that as the family farms sold up many farm auctions would have a horse plough, a wagon and Smyth drill fifty years after they were used.

Steam ploughing at 'Power in the Past,' Wandisden Hall Farm.

Chapter Four

The River Deben from Source to the Sea
From Fresh Water to Salt Water

The freshwater River Deben starts with several streams above Debenham. By the time it flows down Water Lane, Debenham it becomes, in the winter, 'the longest ford in England.'

In about 1970 Cranford Balch and a friend decided to row down the River Deben from Debenham to the tidal river. They first attempted the row when the river was in full flood, thinking there would be more water, but they couldn't get under the bridge just outside Debenham and gave up. The second time, they got as far as Easton, but the whole valley was flooded and they couldn't find the channel and got lost. In the fast-flowing river they were swept into brambles and barbed wire fences and couldn't get under footbridges and overhanging trees.

On their third attempt they picked a day when the river was in partial flood, but they could still find the channel. They also had friends, following by road, who helped them carry the dinghy around the bridges and weirs. They left Debenham at 8.30am and rowed a light fibreglass dinghy down past Brandeston School weir and Letheringham Mill. They had to carry their boat at Wickham Market and Ash Mills and finally arrived at Woodbridge Tide Mill at 5pm.

Another boating activity on the fresh water river in modern times has been the creation of Ufford Sailing Club, a rather informal group meeting at the bar of the 'White Lion' in Lower Ufford. It was started in 2003, with the artist Stuart Atkinson as commodore. One of the club's events is a race from Waldringfield 'Maybush' up to the 'White Lion', but the last part is often done on foot. The club also has a regatta, held, when water allows, on the Foskett's irrigation pond on the other side of the river at Bromeswell.

There has always been speculation about whether there was any barge traffic up the fresh water Deben, but there seems to be no proof that there was ever any commercial traffic on this part of the river. Certainly, once the watermills were built, they would have stopped any sizable river traffic. Weirs were built across the river to create a head of water to drive the mills and the Lords of the Manor jealously guarded their riparian rights to the water.

There were at least eight watermills on the fresh water Deben and one Tide Mill at Woodbridge. However, there were four more watermills on the streams leading into the tidal river – at Bromeswell, Shottisham, Newbourne and on the River Finn, making thirteen watermills. In fact, the river powered the old rural economy. No wonder the landowners fought over the rights to use the water.

Starting at the head of the river there were possibly two small medieval mills above the Kettleburgh Mill. In 1834 the medieval mill at Kettleburgh was replaced by a mill with an undershot wheel. This mill was never a great success as there was just not enough water in the river to drive it. A wind smock mill was moved here in about 1873 to try and give the miller a living. Kettleburgh Mill closed in 1908 and was pulled down in 1937.

The Sanctuary Bridge at Letheringham is the next feature coming down river. After the hard winter of 1947 the snowmelt caused serious flooding in the Deben valley. Around Letheringham this went on for weeks and was so disruptive that farmer Willy Kerr helped to finance the building of Sanctuary Bridge, in about 1949. This replaced a wooden footbridge beside a ford. Because the river was badly silted the channel was dredged out with draglines.

The parish boundary between Letheringham and Easton runs along the course of the old river near Easton Farm Park. When Letheringham Mill was built in 1740 a channel was constructed by hand, to divert the river towards the Almshouses in Letheringham Street. This created a better fall of water to drive the wheel. The wheel was removed from Letheringham Mill in 1927, but in 1990 the owners of the Mill House re-installed a waterwheel and crown wheel.

The new mill channel made it difficult to drain the fields around Letheringham Hall and wooden 'quills' (pipes) were placed under the new channel to drain water into the old river. When John Kerr replaced them in the 1970s plastic pipes were fitted, but they floated up and had to be replaced with steel pipes.

Just down river was an area known as the Fish Ponds near Glevering Mill. This small mill was last used to pump water up to Glevering Hall and has since become a private house. The Deben Mill, at Wickham Market was the most successful water mill on the fresh water river. There was enough water

David Rackham's Deben Mill, at Wickham Market. The Mill House is on the left, then the watermill and former steam mill. The natural river course comes from to the right.

John Fleming of Mill End Farm, Eyke, showing his mare and foal at the Suffolk Show, 2008. At the time John had eleven 'chesnut' Suffolk horses in the Deben valley.

for it to be worked for twenty-four hours most of the year and only in the height of the summer was there a shortage of water. At the Deben Mill, which is first recorded in 1701, it took two and a half hours to grind a ton of wheat. In the small, low powered mills, it must have taken a lot longer.

To improve productivity at the Deben Mill, a windmill nearby was also used for grinding but in 1868 the miller Ephraim Walker had it pulled down and used some of the bricks to build a steam driven mill. Walker got into financial difficulties and in 1885 Reuben Rackham left his farm at Campsea Ash and bought the Deben Mills from the Woodbridge bankers Alexander & Gurney. (Barclays Bank occupies Alexander's home in Church Street.) At the time, cheap food was coming in from the new countries in the Empire and farming was in decline, while country milling gave a better income.

In 1894 Reuben Rackham had a larger roller mill installed and when it was first used his young son, Edward, was lifted up by the foreman so that he could turn it on. Rackham's new mill altered the Deben valley and surrounding villages because they could now produce more flour cheaper than the other wind and watermills. Rackham was soon supplying the small bakeries around Woodbridge, Framlingham, Saxmundham and Aldeburgh and just after World War I Reuben Rackham had a steam lorry to deliver flour to the village bakeries.

In 1957 E.R. & R.T. Rackham, Reuben's sons, had electricity installed to run the roller mill and Robert 'Bertie' Rackham's daughter switched on the power for the first time. The steam engine, which had been kept clean and polished, was given to the Museum of East Anglian Life, at Stowmarket. In the 1950s many of the small village bakeries were put out of business by the larger bakeries and the Rackhams switched to producing flour for Peak Freans, for making biscuits. The roller mill was closed in 1960 when they wanted flour delivered in a bulk lorry and Rackhams found it would have been uneconomic to buy one for a mill of this size.

In 1967 I visited the Deben Mill when 73-year-old Edward Rackham and his brother Bertie were grinding flour for an order from Woodbridge. Since Bertie, who went on to live to be a hundred, had been doing it since 1910 he saw nothing unusual about it. The watermill at the Deben Mill was last used in 1970. When Gordon Holland had an irrigation pond dug just up river it slowed down the water flowing to the mill. By then E.R. & R.T. Rackham had expanded the coal sales, which they had done ever since buying the steam engine, and developed the sales of animal feeds and provender.

During the 1950s two boats were kept above the Deben Mill. The *Lilapet*, a clinker double-ended boat with a sail, and a small rowing boat that were often rowed or paddled up to Glevering. There appear to have been other double-ended boats on the river that were used for angling.

In periods of heavy rain the sluice above the mill was opened and in the Great Flood of 1912, just after Reuben Rackham's wagon had been over it with a ton of flour, the force of water swept away the footings of Wickham Market Bridge. In 1924 and 1947 there was again major flooding in the Deben valley and the other extreme was the very dry summer of 1966. In order to give water to Hayward's cattle, on the marshes, the sluice gates were closed at the Deben Mill. This was the only time that the Rackhams knew of, when the flow of water down to Ash Mill stopped. After this the Environment Agency put in bore holes in Debenham so that in dry summers they could keep a flow going and keep the wildlife alive.

In the 1930s the Rackham brothers rented the mill at Campsea Ash, for three days a week, from the Loudham Estate. The original medieval mill had been built by the Augustinian Canons whose Abbey was founded in 1195 and the millpond had been the monks 'stew pond' where they kept fish for Fridays. The pond was later called the Decoy Pond and used for duck shooting. This mill was known as Ash Abbey Mill or Campsea Ash Mill or more simply called Ash Mill. Although there was only two-foot head of water at the Ash Mill, the high fall of water powered it.

In the summer the Rackhams used to work the Deben Mills in the morning and then Bertie would cycle quickly down to the Ash Mill and use the same water to grind corn there. Rackhams worked this mill until 1956, by which time the corn was mainly being ground for animal food. The mill became a private house known as Loudham Mill.

White Women's Lane in Eyke got its name because women used to walk back from the small water mill, near the ford covered in flour. The small island may have been the site of the mill, but there was no pond and it is difficult to see how it ever accumulated enough water. When John Fleming's grandfather took on their farm in 1908 the water mill was already long gone. There was another small mill that spanned the river at Ufford, on the bend above the road bridge, that stopped work in 1916.

The Abbot of Ely built the first mill at Melton. The creation of Melton Mill was a major undertaking, with part of the river's flow being diverted into a newly dug channel from Ufford Bridge. Mills used to be big business and the miller's houses, after the squires and rectors, were the most impressive in the village. However, these country millers were gradually squeezed out as they could not produce flour as cheaply as the big roller mills on Ipswich Dock. The last miller at Melton gave up and moved to Ipswich in about 1896.

The name Wilford means 'Willow Ford' and this is the place where people from the Sandlings villages crossed to reach Melton and the wider world. Because it was such an important crossing the gallows once stood on the hilltop as a deterrent to crime. The tradition is that there were stepping stones

Roger Clarke ploughing with two Suffolk Horses at Bucklesham Plough Day. Roger says ploughing with horses 'is the best disguise work ever put on'.

here and the first wooden bridge was built in 1535. In 1765 a narrow brick bridge was built and this was replaced in 1939 by the present bridge. Just below the bridge is Wilford Wharf, and later on sailing barges came up here until the early 1930s, bringing in road-making material for the East Suffolk County Council. Tarring all the country roads was a major undertaking, the last ones were done in the 1920s.

The Tide Mill at Woodbridge has become the symbol of the town, but it came very close to being swept away altogether. To work the mill, tidal water was trapped in a pond as it rose and at low tide the water was released to turn the wheel to power the stones. There had probably been a medieval mill on the same site, but Michael Weaver believes that the present mill was built in about 1793.

Incredibly, the Woodbridge Tide Mill was still being worked after World War II and was the last tidal mill working in Britain. Bertie Rackham ran the mill and business until Witnesham farmer John Matthews bought it in 1954. He installed a diesel engine to grind corn for animal food and ran the mill until it closed in 1956.

The Tide Mill and its Granary had been coated in corrugated iron just after World War I, and when it came up for sale in 1968 it looked picturesque rather than being a good investment. I was one of many local people curious about what would happen to this famous old building and went along to the auction at The Old Theatre in Theatre Street. Claude Whisstock, the Deben's leading boatbuilder, who had a few years earlier created the Tide Mill Yacht Harbour out of the old millpond, was very defiant about the mill's future if he bought it. 'It's an eyesore' snorted Claude, voicing the view of most people in the town, 'If I get it, it's coming down!'

He certainly wanted to buy the Tide Mill to join up his boatyard and 'yacht harbour'. (He refused to use the American word marina and having visited St Ives Boat harbour, on the River Ouse, he used their term.)

The eventual owner, with a final bid of around £7,000, was Mrs Jean Gardner. Over breakfast she had been asked by her husband what she would like for her birthday, and had replied that she would like to buy and save the lovely old Tide Mill at Woodbridge. The Gardners gave the dilapidated Mill to a Trust. The Trust restored the Mill, had the whole building raised up because the ground floor was flooding, and opened it to the public in 1972. To preserve a building 'for ever' is a long time and it has required continual support. In 1993 the Tide Mill had 14,919 visitors but the number per year gradually fell and by 2007 was down to 6,919 visitors.

The Granary, where wheat had been stored before milling, was bought by a group of developers from London. They obtained planning permission to add an extra storey to the building and divided it into flats in about 1995 and a rundown industrial part of Woodbridge became a picturesque area being visited by locals and tourists. Soon afterwards the ground floor of the Granary became a café and was renamed the 'Waterfront Cafe' in 2003. In 2004 the Tide Mill Quay was restored for boats to moor alongside.

Claude Whisstock had built up a considerable reputation as a boat builder in a yard beside the Tide Mill Quay. When fibreglass mass-produced yachts appeared in numbers in the late 1960s Claude Whisstock and Frank Knights, in the adjoining much less sophisticated yard, looked at them, thought they 'wouldn't last' and decided to continue building wooden boats. This decision ended serious boat building at Woodbridge, but the number of yachts kept on the River Deben increased every year.

In its last years Whisstock's Boatyard switched to building aluminium hulls, but it eventually closed in 1991. The site continued to be used for boat repair and storage but Whisstock's yard was labelled as a 'redundant boatyard' and property developers tried to use the site for housing. This has been a disaster in Essex, where quaysides have been turned into sterile areas with no connection to boats or even the river itself. Woodbridge people fought to prevent losing the waterside area at Whisstocks and at a public enquiry housing was ruled out. The best possible use for Whisstocks and the waterfront is for boats.

The best known of the Victorian yachtsmen on the Deben was Edward Fitzgerald with his schooner *Scandal* that he sold to Quilter, a successful stockbroker who was a pillar of the local society. Quilter didn't quite have Fitzgerald's sense of humour and renamed the schooner *Sapphire*. Later, after owning several large sailing yachts, Quilter had the 43ton steam yacht *Peridot*, which was kept at Felixstowe Ferry and laid up for the winter in the creek leading to the Bawdsey Fleet. The *Peridot* drew six feet of water and couldn't always get up to Woodbridge.

According to local memory Quilter had his own gate to reach the platform at Woodbridge station and if he was a little late the train was held up for him. This was commuting with style. The *Peridot* anchored in Kyson Pool and when guests came up from London by rail the crew had to carry their luggage, on their backs, down the river wall. Lady Quilter used to stand on the aft deck to receive her guests.

Their destination was Bawdsey Manor, sitting on the cliff overlooking the entrance to the River Deben. The Manor started as a weekend retreat in 1886 and was altered and added to until 1910. Originally the public road went right past Bawdsey Manor, but Quilter had faggots laid on the marshes and created a new road. There were mild local protests at this high-handed action, but no one in the five villages he owned dared to say a word against it.

The only person to raise any objection to the radical changes taking place was Tighe-Gregory, the vicar of St Mary's Church, Bawdsey. The redoubtable Tighe-Gregory, an Irishman in his nineties, had to be carried into church, by his devoted parishioners, on a special chair. Changing the road made little difference to anyone, but Tighe-Gregory ignored the new lodge gatehouse and carried on using the old road near the new Bawdsey Manor. This drove Quilter wild and he tried to have Tighe-Gregory sacked, but the Church of England was very proud of its ancient vicar. Besides, if a vicar had not disgraced himself with a public scandal, there was simply no mechanism to dismiss him. The elderly bishops were certainly not going to dismiss anyone because of old age.

The 'Sorrel Horse', on Shottisham Knoll.

Chapter Five

Alde and Ore
One River Two Names

Old Suffolk is alive and well in the Blaxhall 'Ship'. The 'Orford Boys', the Quay Street Whalers, were singing here in 2008. The year before, Blaxhall fought a passionate campaign to prevent 'The Ship' from being closed.

The Oxblood Molly, of Peasenhall, dancing in Leiston Abbey barn. When the Puritans outlawed dancing the ploughboys used to dress up as women, blacken their faces so that they couldn't be recognized, and continue dancing. Now that it is seen as being politically incorrect to blacken a face, the East Anglian Molly dancers just cover their faces. In East Anglia the plough was the symbol of hope for the future.

What is the original name for the estuary that starts above Snape and runs out at Shingle Street? It begins with a series of freshwater streams running down from central Suffolk. One of these streams is called the Foam and runs down from Saxmundham, while a longer stream called the Alde comes from Rendham and another, the Ore, from Framlingham. Once the water becomes tidal the river becomes the Alde past Snape and Aldeburgh, but just above Orford the name changes to the Ore.

The River Alde below Snape is one of the last estuary wildernesses in eastern Suffolk because it is almost impossible for the general public to get there, except briefly by boat at high tide. Iken Church stands guarding over this stretch of the twisting channel, a peaceful place that was once an island. The thatched church is probably on the site of St Botolph's monastery of Icanhoe, built in about 654 and destroyed by the Vikings in the winter of 869-70.

St. Botolph no doubt chose the island on the Alde to start his mission because there were many Saxon settlements in the area. In 1827 a 'party of gentlemen from London' who came down and 'opened' mounds in the Snape and Blaxhall Common areas destroyed many of the burials without making a record. In 1862 the local landowner Septimus Davidson excavated a group of burial mounds, on the Snape-Aldeburgh road, and discovered they had been robbed, but there had been a longship buried here with a Saxon warrior in it. This longship had probably been brought up Ham Creek that then went around behind Black Heath Wood. Between 1985-91 William Filmer-Sankey,

The tripper boat *Cormorant* going down the River Alde from Snape Maltings, 2008. Snape Maltings is a good example of how something good from the past can be revitalized for the future.

Des Kaliszewski sailing the small spritsail barge *Cygnet* back to Snape Quay.

of the Snape Historical Trust, re-dug the Snape site and discovered a grave with a 10ft log canoe in it. The Snape burial field was a smaller version of the famous Sutton Hoo site.   In 1907, because erosion had revealed Roman pottery, the Aldeburgh Literary Society dug on Barber's Point and believed that it had been a Roman site on an island. Between 2002-06 the Aldeburgh and District History Society, led by Richard Newman, made some test digs to establish more accurate facts.

The conclusion of this investigation was that there had been Roman, and then Saxon settlements here, where water was boiled to extract salt. Salt extraction was a major occupation all along the East Coast and the Iken Reaches, which have large areas of mud flats, were ideal because the sun evaporated the pools left on the mudflats and increased the salt content. There are at least four Red Hills in this reach, sites of former salt workings.

It is possible that the Barber's Point settlement was abandoned when the Vikings raided the Alde and destroyed Botolph's monastery. The remains of Ham Creek ran to the west of Barber's Point. Sam Newton believes that Ham means 'home,' a place where people lived. Lower down the River Ore are the Ham Marshes at the entrance to Barthorp's Creek, below Signal Hill and there is also a Ham River on the Deben in Sutton, behind Methersgate Hall.

The first bridge over the Alde at Snape was there in the 1400s when the Bishop of Norwich gave permission for a hermit to seek alms from anyone crossing over. In 1492 Aldeburgh and Orford were arguing about who should repair Snape Bridge. They could not even agree on the name of the estuary so they were unlikely to see eye to eye over maintaining a bridge. In 1571 Snape was supposed to repair one side and Tunstall the other side. This wooden bridge was replaced with a brick humped-back bridge in 1802 and that lasted until 1960, when the present bridge was constructed.

Snape Maltings was the creation of the enterprising merchant Newson Garrett. He bought the Osborne & Fennell coal business that had been run from sheds on the Tunstall side of Snape Bridge and started to win over the trade in the Saxmundham area. The corn and coal trade on the Alde had been dominated, since the late 1600s, by Mingay, and then Mingay and Rope. They had a granary on stilts at Iken Cliff and a coal yard just down the lane from the 'Anchor'. Mingay and Rope had a fleet of sloops and schooners bringing coal from the north and taking corn to ports all round the southern North Sea. Their vessels sometimes dropped part of their cargo at Boyton Dock, more at Orford and the rest 'up the Cliff'.

It seems that Garrett pushed the Ropes out of the Alde coal trade and purchased their Iken granary, but George Rope continued as a coal merchant at Orford using the quay and warehouses rented from the Sudbourne Estate. Rope's schooners had often drawn 10ft of water loaded, so Iken Cliff had been about their limit. Newson Garrett's other great innovation was building a sailing barge, the *Argo* in 1858, which had a flat bottom and could get up to Snape easily.

Malt, for brewing, had been made on a small scale in the early Victorian period, but malting began to develop into an industrial process. Newson Garrett saw malting as being a business opportunity and between 1846-95 Snape Maltings was expanded. This huge set of industrial buildings, on the edge the Alde marshes, grew to have floor space covering seven acres. Snape was an ideal site because the barley used in malting grew well on Suffolk's light sandy land and there was water transport to ship it off to London breweries. Welsh coal for the kiln fires was brought around by boomies (gaff ketch-rigged barges) from Saunderfoot, which didn't have a railway link.

During the winter malting season about one barge a month was arriving at Snape Maltings, with imported barley from the London docks. It was a very difficult place to reach with a loaded barge – if the wind was against them they took several days to get from Iken Church up to Snape Maltings. They had to kedge and poke their way around the bends, but Alde 'huffers' (pilots) knew all the tricks of the trade in getting a barge up river. 'Jumbo' Ward, the last river pilot, who lived in the cottage overlooking the river at Iken Cliff, remembered Sully's *Phoenician* had come from London in twenty-four hours and even more remarkable, the *Beatrice Maud* had left Great Yarmouth at 6am, run down the coast with a stiff NE wind and had to beat up to Slaughden Quay. The barge had gybed 'all standing' (they didn't shorten sail) going up river and arrived at Snape Quay at 3pm having 'carried' the flood tide the whole way.

After Newson Garrett died in 1893 his son George ran the malting business. He built the New House in 1895 and after this the only major building to go up was the grain silo in 1952. A branch railway line had been constructed down to the Maltings and nicknamed the 'Snape Express', although the little engine barely got up to 20mph. This was closed in 1960.

Snape Maltings was the centre of the world for the villages around and several generations of the same family worked there. It was a major blow when, in 1965, S. Swonnell & Son, who had amalgamated with Garretts in 1919, went into voluntary liquidation and the Maltings were closed. The men working on the malt floors left their shovels and hand tools neatly stacked against the walls and went home shocked. Automated malting had become far cheaper to operate than the Victorian floor maltings, where the malt had been turned daily by hand.

Most people in the Suffolk business world thought Snape Maltings was a white elephant which would be pulled down, but George Gooderham bought it and the 'Plough and Sail' and malsters cottages. George had been running Fazeboons Farm, but saw the Maltings as a storage area for the

The Aldeburgh boat *Enterprise* coming ashore from working on 'The Garden', the fishing grounds just off the town.

Cod, caught on a longline, landed on the Aldeburgh cat *Enterprise*, 2008.

Gooderham and Hayward corn business at Marlesford. George's original plan was to develop Snape Maltings as a port where goods could be shipped in and stored in the buildings. The first barge up there, after a twenty-six year gap since *Beatrice Maud* in 1939, was the *Atrato* in 1965. Jumbo Ward resumed his old career as the pilot and mystified the young motor barge skippers with instructions such as 'luff up around that mark, and then bear away to windward after that'.

The introduction of power craft that churned up the mud allowed the first of Crescent Shipping's larger coastal vessels to get up to Snape in 1967. This was the 103ft 250 ton *Gillation*, with maize from Rotterdam. She drew 8ft and although the tide was ebbing at Iken Cliff, Jumbo took her up to Snape Quay. The imported animal feed was stored on the Malting floors. Once, in the dead of night, there was a deep roar and all the floors in the building nearest Garrett's old home collapsed with 900 tons of fishmeal. Several floors crashed down to ground level and it took weeks to sort out.

The height of Snape's brief re-birth as a port came during the Cold War when the Cobra Mist 'over the horizon early warning radar', paid for by the United States, was constructed on Lantern Marshes. Because of strong protests from Aldeburgh, lorries were not allowed to deliver material through the town, so most of it was shipped through Snape and some goods came in by sea. The contract to deliver the material to Lantern Marshes in 1967 was won by Horlock's of Mistley and their motor barges made several trips a week with about 30,000 tons going down river. Once Horlock's barge *Spithead*, a converted World War I landing craft, was blown around while coming up river and arrived at Snape stern first.

The Cobra Mist opened in 1970, but failed to detect what the Soviets were up to and it closed in

1973. After this the BBC took over the transmission towers and used them for their World Service.

Snape Maltings' future became secure when Aldeburgh Festival took a long lease on the largest malt house overlooking the marshes. After Snape Maltings closed, the Aldeburgh Festival had been interested in developing a concert hall there, but didn't want to buy the whole complex. They took on the New House and, to convert this building, four kilns and three malt floors were removed, some of which had been built with timber taken from broken-up wooden trading vessels.

On June 2, 1967 The Queen and Prince Phillip came and officially opened the new Concert Hall. It was a fairly informal affair outside the main door to the hall, and a bit like the opening of a village fete. Queen Elizabeth II made a short speech but those standing on the wooden bridge couldn't hear. The Duke of Edinburgh tried to jolly the whole thing up by strolling over to a group of Old Age Pensioners, seated in front, and asking them if they were the choir. This got a short, amazed laugh. A select group of the great and the good of the Aldeburgh Festival were very much to the fore, with Benjamin Britten taking the leading role.

We had seen Britten at a management party at the Gooderham's house on April 2. He was just out of hospital and looked frail and red-faced. The leading figures of the Aldeburgh Festival hovered around to make sure that he was not bothered by unwanted attention. He was much better on May 21 when we went to the acoustic test of the new Concert Hall. There was a wonderful aroma of new wood and the proceedings started with Peter Pears saying 'Can you hear me Arthur?' and when a man halfway up the hall said 'Yes', everyone laughed.

Next we all had to be quiet, for the benefit of the Decca sound engineers. After this there were three explosions and we all had to shout 'help' three times. Then a grand piano was pushed on to the stage, the lights dimmed and a short concert followed, with Britten playing the piano and Peter Pears singing. He filled the building with his voice and personality. To begin with, Britten seemed very formal and unsure of himself, but he suddenly changed and became extremely at ease and happy when he saw that everyone was obviously enjoying themselves.

After this, five children from Leiston Secondary School played hand bells and then Phillip Ledger played the piano while Mary Wells sang. There was a magical atmosphere in the auditorium. This was highbrow London culture invading Suffolk, but the audience was thrilled that this could be happening in Snape. Two years later, the night before the Aldeburgh Festival started, the Concert Hall burnt down and it had to be rebuilt. The Queen returned again to reopen the second Concert Hall. In 2007 Aldeburgh Music had their lease extended to 999 years for the whole of New Malt House complex, while the malt floors in the centre, which had been empty since the 1960s, began further development as flats. In 1971 the Gooderhams had opened the Craft Shop on the Quay, which was the first of a series of retail outlets in Snape Maltings.

The great red brick Maltings came to be the cultural centre of Sandlings Suffolk. These warm red bricks give coastal Suffolk its architectural character. Only Aldeburgh and Covehithe brickworks survive but there used to be many other places in the Sandlings with brickworks. Leiston brickworks closed in 1921 and Snape not long afterwards. There had been brickworks at Orford, Tunstall, Melton, Hacheston, Sutton, Hollesley and Alderton, among others. In the eighteenth century, when the timber-framed Suffolk longhouses were no longer being built, most new houses and cottages were built of Suffolk red brick, with gently arched windows and door tops, and sometimes a brick course slightly above the roof.

Aldeburgh Brickworks originally sent away most of its output by barge. When Walter Riggs owned the brickworks, he had the barge *Alde* built on Slaughden Quay in 1882. Jumbo Ward, the river pilot, told me in 1968 that Eastwood's barges *Cheshire*, *Lancashire* and *Bedford* were built to load bricks at the end of the Aldeburgh Brickworks' jetty. The wagons of bricks went down from the kilns on a tramway and boys used to ride down on the wagons to pull the hand brake on when they reached the quay. If they were too late they went over the end. A horse used to pull the trucks back up again.

Orford still has a commercial quay used by fishing and passenger boats. The *Lady Florence* runs river cruises and open launches take passengers down to Havergate Island, across to Orfordness 'The Island' and on river trips around Havergate.

Orford was the port for the Sudbourne Hall Estate, which extended between Snape and the Butley River.

In the inter-war years, the two decades between the World Wars, road transport began to change the whole way of life in the countryside. There was a huge surplus of narrow gauge railways, which had once served the trenches on the Western Front. In 1928 a narrow gauge railway was built on Orfordness to take material to the Government's research station there. In 1911 Hollesley Bay Colony had been bought by the Central Unemployment Committee to rehabilitate the poor from London. They laid a tramway from the Colony Dock across the marshes to the main buildings. Barges brought in horses' muck, and even rags, which were taken in horse drawn trucks to their new 'gardens.'

While most barge quays were called Docks, the Colony Dock, because of the strong tide, was a complete enclosed concrete dock. By 1940 the entrance to the River Ore was almost opposite the Colony Dock, but it moved south and most of the dock was swept away.

On the coast there was another tramway from East Lane towards Shingle Street. The Quilter Estate had a 'beach gang' that maintained the groynes and re-established the beach when shingle was washed away. Once, when the sea broke through, a barge was towed around from Ipswich, sunk in the gap, and then shingle piled around it.

Aldeburgh enjoys modest fame in maritime history circles as being the last port to have smacks with wet wells that went longlining for cod in the North Sea. In the medieval period Dunwich and Ipswich also sent ships north as far as Iceland in search of cod, and brought them back salted. Later, sailing smacks adopted the Dutch practices of keeping cod alive in wet wells. In the late nineteenth century trawlers replaced longlining smacks, but Aldeburgh and Harwich didn't have the capital to invest in steam trawlers so they continued to use old sailing smacks.

Aldeburgh smacks spent most of their time working out of Harwich; it was easier to get their catch to London from there. The crews used to walk home, across the ferry to Felixstowe, over another ferry to Bawdsey, on again on foot to Butley ferry and finally had to ring the bell on the Sudbourne shore for the Slaughden ferryman to come and get them. The last sailing smack longlining was Aldeburgh's *Gypsy* in 1913. Launched in 1882, she had probably been the last smack built at Slaughden.

In the 1920s the people at Orford were very amused when a salesman appeared on the Quay and demanded to know when the next ferry went down to the village of Havergate Island. He had been told to go to every village, but never got to Havergate! Havergate, pronounced Haverg'ut, is nearly two miles long and has 265 acres behind the river walls. It was a parish in its own right, even though the only inhabitants were the two marsh men and their families, who were in charge of the cattle.

The marshes along the East Coast rivers, although not very interesting to sail past, were a vital part of the rural economy and it must have taken a vast investment to reclaim them. The river walls were put up by hand labour, and in the case of the area from Sudbourne to the Orford Town Marshes this meant putting up a wall four miles long. This had to be done because the grass on the top land died off in the summer and the farmers had no food for their animals. The grass on the marshes went on growing because there was a high water table.

Cattle were driven in through Aldeburgh to graze the Lantern Marshes, but were forced to swim across to Orfordness or Havergate until a small flat-bottomed barge was used. There were ridges and furrows in the marshes on Havergate that showed wheat had once been grown. When Harry Fiske of Bramford, just outside Ipswich, owned the island it was all grass. The cattle were driven (walked) by road to a field near Melton Church on the first night and then on to Orford the next day. Fiske sold Havergate in 1917, and Oxley, which is behind Shingle Street, to the Hollesley Bay Colony in 1940. Cattle then came by rail to Saxmundham and were driven down to graze on Havergate marshes.

The marshes were often owned or rented by farmers from inland villages. On the seaward end of the Deben the marshes were drained by the Bawdsey Fleet and divided between the farms on the Sandlings Peninsula. After the 1953 flood, farming practices altered on the East Coast marshes. The Government put pressure on farmers to plough them up and grow wheat, when the salt had been washed out of the land, and this was very successful. Irrigation ponds were also dug on the low ground and this enabled the Suffolk coastal area to be suitable for growing vegetables, now the area's major industry. The Sandlings have a maritime climate, milder, without late frosts, and this allows crops to grow about two weeks earlier in the spring and they go on growing for about a week longer in the autumn.

In the 1980s, wheat prices failed to keep up with costs and many marshes were reverted back to grass, for animal grazing. The Royal Society for the Projection of Birds bought Havergate Island, because avocets were found nesting here in 1947, and this opened up the area for 'bird tourism'. People had been coming out of the towns to shoot pheasants and partridge on the Suffolk heathlands and marshes, but after the RSPB purchased the island even more arrived, just to watch the birds.

At one time Havergate must have been part of Gedgrave (pronounced Ged'gruve) Marshes, but by 1530 the Gull, a channel around the back of the island, formed and made Havergate an island. Gull in Suffolk usually means small drainage channel so presumably it started off small and got larger. The Butley River had flowed out into Hollesley Bay until about 1575 when the ever-growing Orfordness extended past it.

Maria Smith, mother of ten, lived in the Ferry House and used to operate the ferry at Butley. In 1932 the fare was two pence each way, but some time later the boat was damaged when it got jammed in the sluice on a high tide. The ferry was abandoned and the house pulled down.

In 1993 Bryan Rogers had 20 tons of hardcore put down to repair the landing hard and restarted

Butley Ferry on the Butley River with Graham Hussey on the right.

The Suffolk beach boat *Three Sisters* at the top of Barthorp's Creek in 2006. The road bridge is on the route to Shingle Street.

the ferry, but there were few passengers and he gave up. In 2002 the Alde and Ore Association reopened the Butley Ferry with volunteer ferrymen and, mainly through the dogged enthusiasm of Graham Hussey, it has kept running at weekends in the summer. Butley Mill, at the head of the Butley River, was last used to grind corn commercially in 2001. The brick watermill was built in about 1810, to replace an older mill, which again had replaced a medieval mill which had stood on the fresh water stream, about two miles further inland, near Staverton Park.

Butley Mill produced wholemeal flour until 1914 and then switched to producing animal feed. Eventually an engine was used for grinding the corn instead of the waterwheel. While Butley Mill was renowned for producing chicken and pony food, about ninety percent of its output went in to feeding the Massey's breeding pig herd at Hill Farm, Chillesford. In 2001 swine fever wiped out Massey's pig herd so they had the Mill converted into five holiday flats.

Just before the entrance to the River Ore a tiny creek leads off into the Hollesley shore. This is the remains of Hollesley Haven that probably once ran up towards Hollesley Church. It is on the map as Barthorp's Creek, named after the family who sold the Red House Estate to the Colonial College in 1887.

In the 1970s an instructor from the Borstal at Hollesley Bay was taking canoes up Barthorp's Creek when a paddle struck something solid in the shallows. This turned out to be a skeleton in the mud that was later identified as being a boy who had run away from the Borstal in 1939. Two young men had broken out and one had been recaptured later and taken back. It was assumed that the other boy had 'made a clear break' and got away forever, but in fact he had met a terrible end in the soft mud of the creek.

The marshes in front of Hollesley (pronounced Hoe's'ley) appear to have been walled off in the Elizabethan period, and Oxley became a marsh island. Since Oxley means Ox Island this was presumably where they put the oxen to graze in early times. The hamlet of Shingle Street came later. The settlers built single storey cottages, largely out of timber that had been washed ashore from wrecks and lost cargoes.

The Shingle Street men picked up an income by piloting, fishing, wildfowling and helping to load the barges with shingle. They had special wheelbarrows for walking up a plank. Although never rich, they were their own bosses and had plenty to eat. It was a life that people were attracted to and the number of houses at Shingle Street increased. When Francis Langmaid, a young pilot, made a lucrative salvage of a ship in trouble, he used the money to build the 'Lifeboat Inn', a prefabricated building that had been brought around from Ipswich by barge and unloaded on the beach.

No doubt the Coastguards were good customers at the 'Lifeboat'. The Coastguard Cottages, with the Officer's House on the southern end, were built in 1881. In the late Edwardian era there was a tragic accident off Shingle Street when five coastguards were drowned in the entrance channel, in front of their wives and families. Only one body was recovered. The Coroner for the Liberty of St. Etheldreda recorded that the Coastguard cutter had been to Aldeburgh to collect stores and pay, and left at about 5.15pm, but there was little wind and progress was slow. They stopped at Orford for half an hour and then pressed on down river, stopping at the Victorine Hut to phone up Shingle Street, to see what the state of the sea was at the river mouth. They wanted to take the cutter back to its normal berth on the beach in front of the house but were told 'don't come out of the river on any account', as there was not enough water on the bar and the sea was too bad. However the officer decided he was going to put the cutter back on the beach and haul it up to unload the stores.

It was dusk when they reached the entrance and the tide was so strong that the cutter couldn't stay on course. They lowered the sail and mast and started to row as hard as they could, but the cutter was swept into the breakers and capsized. Only two of the crew of seven managed to get ashore on the shingle knoll, but it was then dark. Two of the Coastguards from the station then launched the pilot boat, rowed across the river and rescued the two men. A verdict of accidental death was brought in, no doubt because the officer in charge was one of those drowned.

During World War II the Suffolk coast was in the front line for much of the time. There were aerial battles fought overhead, and often sea fights as well. At some point burned bodies of men were washed up on Shingle Street beach. At the same time several bodies were also found on the beaches at Aldeburgh and along the coast to Southwold. No one knew where they had come from, but at the time it was not thought to be unusual.

Earlier in the war, during the Dunkirk Evacuation, the exploding shells had been seen clearly from Bawdsey. It seems likely that one night in September 1940, when the RAF bombed the oil tank storage area at Dunkirk, the flash from the explosions, deflected by the Sirius cloud, were seen on the Suffolk coast.

After the war, Hammond Innes wrote a novel about Germans landing at Shingle Street and this seems to have started the ball rolling for a legend that German troops had landed at Shingle Street and been repelled by British troops. Over the decades a story grew up that the Germans had landed at Shingle Street and had been destroyed by British soldiers setting fire to oil on the sea. The legend was fuelled by a television programme, two books, a website and letters to the *East Anglian Daily Times* with accounts by people who thought they might have seen or heard something, but never eye witnesses

At the beginning of World War II the civilian population were still living at Shingle Street. The pilot for the entrance of the River Ore, Eric Andrews, was looking out at the river once when he saw a drifting mine. Thinking this was dangerous he launched his boat off the beach, went out and put a rope on the mine and towed it into the entrance of the river. He got ashore, went over a ridge in the beach, and was driving a stake in to fasten his catch, when the mine exploded.

This is the only wartime incident that Eric Andrews was involved in. In 1940 everyone was moved out of Shingle Street and most of the beach was mined. The Shingle Street residents were only moved as far as Hollesley, so they could still see Shingle Street across the marshes and some of them witnessed the experimental bomb being dropped on the hamlet in 1943, destroying the 'Lifeboat'. During the rest of the war the Suffolk coast was a military zone and the Army and the RAF occupied Shingle Street at different times. Ray Jacobs recalled that Leslie Walker, who was invalided out of the army, was sent to Shingle Street as a Coastguard. He saw a large area of burnt grass where flame-throwers were tried out and some soldiers had been injured.

In 1940 the Government organized 'Cromwell Day' as a full-scale rehearsal to repel an invasion. This brought out the weaknesses in Britain's anti-invasion plans, but it had been an poorly organized exercise and not everyone realized it had been a rehearsal. When John Warwicker researched for evidence to see if there was any truth in the legend about Germans landing at Shingle Street he discovered that the story could have originated from our own Government. With German troops amassing around Calais the Government had put out misinformation that the British Army could 'set fire' to the sea. It was a desperate attempt to try and persuade the Nazi leaders that terrible harm would come to them if they tried to invade. Numerous propaganda stories were 'leaked' to confuse the enemy.

In 1942 there were unsuccessful experiments involving pouring oil on the sea to set it on fire, but not on the East Coast. The Germans had already experimented with this idea in the Baltic, also with a total lack of success. It is doubtful if the Germans took much notice of these carefully planned rumours. They were much more concerned that they had failed to get control of the skies in the Battle of Britain. If they had wanted to make a landing on British soil they would have tried landing in Kent, Sussex or even some other open part of the Suffolk coast. They certainly would not have picked a difficult place such as Shingle Street, which would have meant coming inshore between the offshore sandbanks and exposing themselves to attack from the air and coastal ships at Harwich.

After the war the Government let it be known that some 'news items' had in fact been propaganda hoaxes. Many people then jumped to the conclusion that this was a 'cover up' to hide very dark secrets. People who had moved into the area loved the stories of a 'German Invasion' and refused to allow the rumour to die. Local people remained mystified by this rumour without real foundation. My father, Norman Simper, was in the Observer Corp, taking night shifts, either on Screwsmore Common, Shottisham, or in a scaffold pole tower on the high ground at Alderton. They were in touch with other units and at no time did he hear of a German raid or anything remotely similar.

Fifty years after World War II, John Gummer MP got the official Government papers released and there was virtually nothing about Shingle Street. In 2004 BBC Radio did a major research project and came to the final conclusion that nothing of importance had happened at Shingle Street during World War II. The real mystery about Shingle Street is why there was ever a mystery in the first place.

Ed Daniell holding the Friesian team pulling the hearse with Mike Daniell driving at a funeral at Wickham Market

Mike Daniell at the Poplar Park Equestrian Centre, Hollesley grooming his Friesian horses at the end of a working day.

Chapter Six

Defending the Realm
The North Sea Battle

Shingle Street was literally a 'street' of shingle in front of the original single storey cottages. Because Shingle Street was linked by a track on the beach to the East Lane fishermen's hamlet, it comes under the parish of Bawdsey.

Ramsholt Dock was built for barges to bring coal in and take coprolite out. The coprolite was dug from local pits and turned into fertilizers in Ipswich. Hay and straw were taken to London for the street horses. Wallers, local landowners, probably built the present quay in about 1870 with profits from coprolite pits. Cargoes ended with sugar beet in the 1920s and it then became derelict and half washed away. It was rebuilt in 1957 for yachts.

I first made contact with the sea in about 1947 when my grandmother Turner decided to buy a beach hut at The Dip in Felixstowe. The houses of Felixstowe now extend down to the road near The Dip but then fields backed it. In summer the sloping shingle beach below the huts used to be crowded with children paddling and swimming in the sea. On rainy days we sat in the hut with flasks of tea and cucumber sandwiches. My grandmother used to occupy the pole position and my mother and various aunts and cousins grouped around. I don't remember the male members of the family joining us much, but when my father did come he quickly got bored of sitting around, and suggested that we should go on a trip around the Cork lightship on Ford's tripper boat. This was my first experience of going to sea. The Fords, who had originally had a fishing boat on Bawdsey beach, kept their open boat at Felixstowe Ferry and on fine days brought her round to take trips from a stage at The Dip.

In calm weather we actually went aboard the Cork Lightship, and the lightship men were given a tip. Once, on the trip back, the weather deteriorated and became very rough but I was reassured by one of the Fords, at the tiller, who said quite calmly 'it's wind over the tide'. This all seemed very exciting and these were happy times.

On very low tides people used to swim out to rocks, just off the beach, which had once been the inner wall of Walton Castle. From Roman times a headland has gone into the sea here and a concrete wall has since been constructed to prevent the sea's relentless progression inland. The Dip looks like a military area nowadays; all very different from my distant youth, but if the wall had not been built the beach huts and houses on the clifftop would have already gone into the sea. The Suffolk coast is under attack from the North Sea, an enemy that gives no mercy.

In one lifetime parts of the coast can alter out of recognition. If the seamen who sailed the Sutton Hoo Ship some 1,400 years ago returned, they would simply not recognize the coast at all. Headlands and huge sections of the coast have gone and rivers have silted up with the soil being dragged south. There is no natural coast, the sea just eats all it can and never stops trying.

On a high tide in a north-easterly gale, huge waves come thundering in up the beaches and wash away the soft cliffs. The offshore banks should prevent waves larger than 25ft high from reaching the coast, but offshore dredging for ballast is in serious danger of removing this natural protection. Without proper protection, some seventeen towns and villages along the Suffolk coast are all under threat of going into the sea. After them, the next seventeen will go in time. This does sound extreme, but remember Dunwich and its wonderful harbour vanished in the medieval period, and much of Covehithe, Easton Bavents and Slaughden have gone. The loss of this land was tragic to the people who lived here. In an age of rapidly rising population, land for people to live, and grow food on, must be among our number one priority.

Most of Southwold and Aldeburgh would have already disappeared without sea defences, and so would much of Felixstowe and Lowestoft. In the twentieth century, engineers became very good at sea defences but a far larger problem appeared – Government apathy.

High tide at Ramsholt Dock, November 9, 2007. There were major high tides on the East Coast in 1734, 1897 and 1953 and again a high tide in September 1968, but this time the sea defences held. Major flood warnings went out for the November 9 2007 tide, but fortunately the low-pressure tidal surge that moved down the North Sea didn't coincide with the high tide.

Ramsholt Dock quay under water, 2007. There is nothing unusual about high tides putting some of the quays on the Deben, Ore and Alde and the road bridge to Shingle Street under water. The land and settlements recover from high tides and inland flooding, but erosion takes away our heritage forever.

East Lane, Bawdsey, 2008. These are the only buildings left after the Boathouse Point and houses on it went into the sea about 1911.

Looking from the car park near The Dip, Felixstowe across the mouth of the River Deben, 2005. All the land in the foreground would have gone into the sea, if sea defences had not been carried out in the past century.

Vic Clouting and Dick Graham spinning for bass in the strong tide on the Bawdsey Manor end of the shingle bar at the Deben entrance.

Once you are half a mile from the sea, beyond the sound of the breaking waves, erosion really doesn't seem a problem, but the menacing tidal water is still there. The Government ministers who sit comfortably behind their desks in London, are well aware that erosion and rising sea levels are a major national problem, but it is all happening very slowly. Each Government only has to keep bluffing their way for five years. By spending a little money on endless, pointless reports they appear to be 'looking into the problem' without actually coming up with a real plan for defending England. What is very naughty is the use of a Government agency, Natural England, to invent reasons to stop sea defences and actually prevent people from defending their own property.

The worst case of this was when Peter Boggis and Charles England were stopped from defending their homes against the encroaching sea at Easton Bavents. It took several years and a High Court ruling to overturn this disruptive action. Not that this seems to have discouraged Natural England, because in 2008 they quite happily suggested that twenty-five square miles of East Norfolk, five villages, could be abandoned to 'make way for water' and allow the sea to move five miles inland. Unbelievable!

The Suffolk coast is dotted with the remains of military installations, constructed to keep out our foes of the past, the French, Germans and the Russians. If any of these had attempted to take some of our homeland, men and women would have fought and died to save it. Yet our own Government is happily prepared to lose huge areas of the coast, without any fight. No one has to lose their life in the battle with the North Sea, but it is a battle, which has to be fought if we are all going to go on living in lowland East Anglia.

Near East Lane, Bawdsey 2004. Posts, the remains of groynes can just be seen in the distance. These used to hold the beach in place, which lessened the impact of waves, but were not maintained. The modern 'rock armouring' seems to allow the waves to crash through and suck out the soil behind.

Near East Lane, Bawdsey 2008. The sea was held back at Bawdsey for decades, but the false economy of not keeping up groynes allowed the sea to tare away the beach and start moving inland.